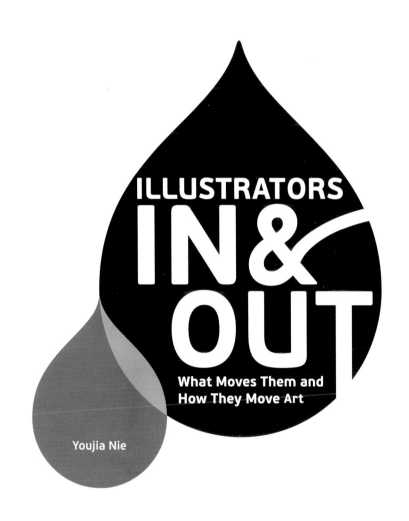

ILLUSTRATORS
IN&
OUT

**What Moves Them and
How They Move Art**

Youjia Nie

CYPI PRESS

CONTENTS

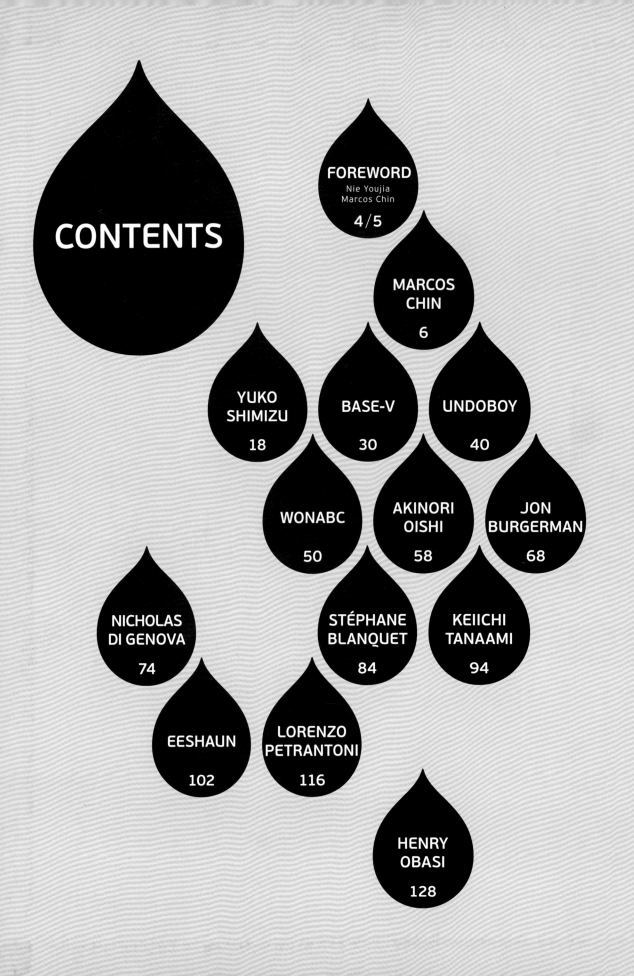

FOREWORD

With the integration between art and commerce, the boundary between high art and pop culture has gradually obscured, and the artists' identity has become more complicated. Amidst this conflict, they are striving for a balance between freedom and commercial trends to generate a burst of energy, which is a positive and feasible approach in this age.

What will happen when illustration as a unique artistic form meets the overall artistic context? For long, illustration seems to be concerned with individualized subject, uncomplicated approach, as well as trendy and easy contents. The red carpet to the art palace is never accessible to illustration. However, today's illustrators can depend on diversified and life-oriented media, as well as individualized and trendy expressive modes which has maximized the values of illustration art to an unprecedented extent by facilitating the integration of illustration, fashion and other industries. Illustration industry has already become an established artistic form, making impressive performance in both artistic and commercial domains. It is due to its close relationship with the public that illustration boasts high commercial values, which is the essential reason for its prevalence in this age. It might be said that illustration art is still gaining ground in the commercial market.

This book showcases works by big names in the contemporary illustration profession, who have already stricken a balance between arts and commerce. On one side, illustrators have strived to give expression to their individuality, manifesting their earnest, passions and insistence through their works. On the other hand, their commercial success also demonstrates how profoundly illustration art has influenced the life. Actually, there is no point in exploring the essence of illustration from the so-called commercial or artistic perspective. No matter which perspective we adopt, the ultimate objective is to demonstrate the joy and happiness in life. That is enough!

I want to express sincere thanks to Marcos Chin from the US and Keiichi Tanaami from Japan. As establised artists in this profession, they have inspired us with their ethics and personality. It is hoped that readers can obtain some enlightenments through this book. It is not expected that they will get a profound understanding or find certain solutions. As long as they can approach illustration art with an earnest heart, this book will be rewarding enough.

Nie Youjia, Art Director of *Cosmopolitan*, China

Why I Draw

When I used to sit in class and listen to my Fiction Writing Professor talk about the process of writing, my mind would often drift; not in a way where I failed to hear what he was saying, but I started to align his words alongside my craft of drawing and illustration. I have a terrible time with labels, assigning and boxing things neatly (or not....) into some kind of space and then calling it a name. I interchange the words, art, and craft, and illustration, and design, and drawing because I'm starting to see them more and more each time as being extremely similar to one another in a sense that they share so many of the same traits. Trying to clinically delineate the difference between each of these disciplines is no longer important to me.

When I was thirteen years old, I clearly remember saying out loud that I wanted to draw for a living. Back then I had no clue what I was talking about because I didn't know anyone who made money from their drawings. When my family and I moved to Toronto, my father worked in a factory and my mother did data entry at her first and only job for decades. Drawing was not practical in their eyes, and as a result I could not foresee that it would take care of me either.

There were moments when I thought that I would give up on drawing. In my third year of Art College I almost dropped out even before the semester began. I wanted to – needed - to move out of my parents' home, and so I considered that I would remain working full time at a clothing factory to save up enough money for rent. Had I done so, I have no clue where I would be now. Fortunately , I snapped out of this delusion of mine, and with the help of my brother and sister, stayed in school for the remaining years, and then moved out shortly after. During this time, I probably drew more fiercely than ever because I guessed that at moment, that I had no other choice. In a way, I cast all of my hopes and frustrations into this particular discipline, desperately hoping it to lift me out of the place that I was in.

I drew some more.

I sometimes look at my drawings and wonder if they are good or not. I understand that if someone else has commissioned the drawing then there are reasons that make it successful. This is when the traditional rules of illustration come into play. The picture needs to communicate an idea and have a concept in order to satisfy a viewership. I know all of this, I believe it, and I teach this to my students: content is paramount. But when I distance myself from my work and really stare at it, subject matter and content together, the parts of it that are not so good begin to reveal themselves to me. I have always fantasized about being a great artist, like the ones whose books I keep on my shelf. They are the ones who are able to manage shape and line in such a way that makes me feel that they have exclusive ownership of them; they employ color with such beautiful ease, as though they were the ones who gave birth to them. But I know that for many of these individuals, or so I say to myself, that I don't believe all of this came easily for any of them. Neither did it come quickly.

I recently opened up Charley Harper's book, the one that was put together by Todd Oldham, and it makes me feel good because the pictures in it reminded me - reminds me - of why I draw. The photos of Harper's work span his entire lifetime, showing images of drawing as the content. The way in which he relates colors to one another is magical and the restraint that he holds in his brush when rendering the details of the figures and objects convinces me that there is a reason and place for every mark that he puts down. And even though he is one of those artists who I have come to revere, I am learning to appreciate the work that he has done as just that, work that he has done. I try to remind myself now of the importance of the act of drawing, drawing for drawing's sake, not drawing for money's sake, nor for the sake of fame, nor for the sake of trying to be like anyone else. These things grow less important to me.

And so I draw.

I draw because I enjoy simply moving the paint around on the page, and stylus on the tablet. I enjoy mixing colors and arranging them next to each other to create patterns. I enjoy making marks on the pages and allowing them to twist and turn into something figurative or abstract. I draw because I have things that I want to say that I might not be able to express through words, or through actions. I draw because when I do, the world around me fades away. I draw because it makes me feel good.

Marcos Chin, Illustrator

MARCOS CHIN

Marcos is known as one of the best-known illustrators in North America. His regular clients include some prominent media such as *Times*, *New Yorker*, and *Rolling Stone*. He has been awarded by the Association of Illustrators (AOI) and Society of Illustraotrs for several times. His illustrations brim over with grace and wisdom, romance and refinement, enveloped in mists of mystery and surging with intricate emotions. Marcos is amazingly talented in use of color, capable of distinguishing and managing a surprisingly wide range of color. His works feature delicate and rich layers of color, emanating a gentleness. His inspirations are based upon his acute observation of his surroundings. Marcos believes that illustration is nothing more than a visual vocabulary an artist constructs on the foundation of his own knowledge and interests.

1 **When did you make up your mind to work as an illustrator? What happened then?**

I decided that I wanted to become an Illustrator while I was in my second year of art college. I admit that it was not a serious pursuit initially, only that it was the one subject in school that aligned with my love of drawing. However, as time progressed, and I became a senior, I realized that this is what I wanted to do, to draw and paint, to tell stories with the pictures that I created, and to publish these images in books and magazines and advertisements. My push to achieve these things was not, and is still not, easy by any means; however, I put so much effort in trying to continue to improve my artistic skills and to embrace the business component of my art that this can sometimes become the most difficult and tedious part of my profession.

2 **Please summarize your design concept. What has contributed to your current style?**

There are so many things that have influenced my work. At the beginning of my career, I was fascinated only by visuals. I didn't care so much about the idea behind the work or the story that was being told – what interested me was how technically skilled the person who created the picture was; and so I tried my best to mimic that quality within his work. However, as I grew older my artistic practice began to shift and I started to become more intrigued by people's ideas and the process that they go through in order to create their work. Essentially, as I change and grow as a person, these qualities are mirrored in my work.

3 **Where do you usually find the inspirations for your works? In other words, what do you usually do in the stage of design?**

When I begin working, I usually like to be out of the studio if I can – if not then I will sit in a chair in my studio that is away from my main workspace; there's a plant by the window along with two small stools, one on which I can rest my coffee or tea, and the other where I can rest my feet. I spend up to a couple of hours loosely sketching out ideas without any sort of research or reference. Afterwards, I change locations and go onto the computer to further enhance my brainstorming process with photo research. I may type in some words that relate to whatever it is that I am trying to illustrate and see what images result from this. This helps me to get outside of myself; to see how others may view, or reinterpret the same subject matter.

4 **What do you think of the relationship between the artistic value and commercial value of the illustrations?**

I do not necessarily think that everything that is artistic has commercial value. This idea really depends on the notion that the picture that is being created, for example, has some sort of audience who is willing to participate with the message it delivers. The intention of commercial work is never art for art's sake, the root word of commercial is "commerce" the activity of buying and selling, therefore, the intention is: art for the sake of making money, and the ability to engage the viewer to alter his or her behavior in favor of the content of the picture quantifies if an image is commercial or not.

5 **Have you found any conflict between drawing for your own fun and doing a commissioning work? How do you think the commercial operation has promoted this artistic creation?**

No, I would not say there is any conflict between the two. If I am providing an illustration for an article then I have to abide by the content of that article, rather than veer off into another artistic direction. As a result, I place utmost importance on getting my commercial work done before I even consider working on self-initiated projects; without the former, I cannot do the latter.

6 **Nowadays, how can an illustrator be successful both in the artistic sense and the commercial sense? Do you have any experience to share with us?**

I believe that if I create work that I like, and enjoy my process in doing so then naturally it will attract (commercial) projects that are similar in terms of concepts and aesthetics towards me. In this sense, even though I am working on a commercial piece it will still be fun to do.

Title: **Japan Groove**
Client: *Time*, Asia

Zbigniew Brzezinski:
Why the World Must
Stand Up for Georgia

The Great
American
Yard Sale

A Candid Talk with
Taiwan Leader
Ma Ying-jeou

TIME

Japan Gets Fresh

A new generation
of Japanese
entrepreneurs is
building a global
reputation for style
and innovation—
by returning to the
country's roots

BY HANNAH BEECH

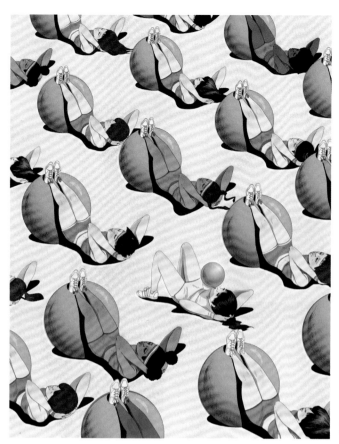

1 2
|
3

7 **As an illustrator, how do you interpret the role you are playing?**

I see myself as someone who provides another way of (re)presenting the world.

8 **What's your icon in the artistic arena? What is the ultimate artist ideal to you?**

When I was younger and in art college, this was a lot easier to answer because I had less experience. Back then, I wanted to just get my work published in magazines, for it to be seen on billboards by the public; and although I still want to continue to have those things happen, I also would like for my work to somehow describe those beliefs of mine, my experiences, and the stories of my own choosing. This is incredibly difficult to achieve because it means that the type of work might not be commercially well received, but I would like for it to be. This is one of my ultimate goals, to align my personal work with my commercial work such that I can live comfortably off it.

9 **In what way do you think the illustration industry has changed? What do you think of the future trends in this industry?**

I think that illustration is tending more towards entrepreneurship and collaboration with other creative individuals in various disciplines. It's no longer about illustrators being circumscribed within a "craft" type of discipline; serving industries as hired hands. Illustrators nowadays are venturing off the printed page and are becoming more "art-oriented," as opposed to "craft- driven," where there are more and more illustrators who are primarily responsible for realizing and/or collaborating the entire vision of their work from start to finish.

1
Title: **Falling Off the Workout Wagon**
Client: **Hers**
2
Title: **Spring Love**
Client: **The Walrus**
3
Title: **Why I Think Soccer is Silly**
Client: **Annabelle**

1
Title: **Finding the Best Provider**
Client: **Plansponsor**
2
Title: **Hooked Up**
Client: **Complex**
3
Title: **Karma**
Client: **Dose**
4
Title: **Hip Twist**
Client: **Maxalot**

1

2 3

1
Title: **12 Days**
Personal Work
2
Title: **Untitled**
Client: **Dellas Graphics**
3
Title: **Cold**
Client: **Terrorismo Graphico, for Diesel Buenos Aires**

1	
2	3

1
Title: **The Big Ask**
Client: **Women's Health**

2
Title: **White Camel**
Client: **Camel**
Advertising Agency: **Coyne, Beahm, Shouse**

3
Title: **Nature Boy**
Client: **Runner's World**

YUKO SHIMIZU

Born in Japan but brought up in New York, Yuko Shimizu has a surprisingly large number of globally-based clients, including "Rolling Stone" and M.A.C. Her works make active presence in *New York Times*, *Playboy*, *The Times*, and so on. Being one of the most commercially successful illustrators at our time, she had a relatively late start as a professional, but soon stood out in this circle due to her professional communication skills and oriental Ukiyoe style. Unexpectedly, Yuko claims that illustration no longer interests her after working thirty years as a professional illustrator. Rather, it is nothing but a job which requires logic and consistency. However, she is still admired for her perserverence as well as the lasting power of her works.

1 **When did you make up your mind to work as an illustrator? What happened then?**

I have always wanted to be an artist, ever since I was in kindergarten. But actually I didn't really make up my mind till I was around thirty years old. Back then I was working as one of the PR staff in a big corporation in Tokyo, Japan.

Job itself wasn't bad, but I strongly felt that this was not what I wanted for the rest of my life. So after a long contemplation I finally made up to do two things I had been wanting to do:

1) to study art for the first time, and eventually become an artist;
2) move to New York.

And that's what I did.

2 **Please summarize your design concept. What has contributed to your current style?**

The concept of each work is determined by the project and/or the assignment.

Because I am an illustrator, my job is to materialize the concept of the project I am given. But for each project I work on, I try to create as honestly to myself and the way I think as possible.

Work evolves naturally. Everything I have ever experienced in my life has contributed to what I do now.

3 **Where do you usually find the inspirations for your works? In other words, what do you usually do in the stage of design?**

People often think that we, illustrators, come up with our images in the way a light bulb turns on. This does sometimes happen, but often ideas don't come that easily.

Once I have a project going on, I do thorough research on the subject matter. Ideas come from understanding. It is a very methodical and logical process.

4 **What do you think of the relationship between the artistic value and commercial value of the illustrations?**

People often ask me what the difference between fine art and illustration is. My answer is the use and context.

Fine art is something that is usually shown in galleries and actual pieces are sold to be shown on someone's home walls, offices or museums, while illustrations are intended to be printed in magazines or on a product, etc.

Nowadays, aesthetically, the border between fine art and illustration is becoming more and more obscure. But difference in usage definitely exists. To cut a long story short, illustration is called illustration because of the nature of its balance between artistic and commercial value.

5 **Have you found any conflict between drawing for your own fun and doing a commissioning work? How do you think the commercial operation has promoted this artistic creation?**

Ideally I should be doing more "drawings for fun," but unfortunately I don't have a lot of time to do so.... Commissioned work gets better when you have time to experiment in your personal work. Paid work is paid work, and they need to be of a certain quality, and it is often very hard to do experimentation with them. Experiment is the way for artists to find new ways of working, finding out new direction, and it is absolutely indispensable.

6 **Nowadays, how can an illustrator be successful both in the artistic sense and the commercial sense? Do you have any experience to share with us?**

I believe it is always important to be who you are and never try to be anyone else. As long as we keep that in mind it really doesn't matter if it is commercial or personal.

7 **As an illustrator, how do you interpret the role you are playing?**

The illustrator's job is to illustrate the idea, story or concept in the best way possible. Please refer to question No.2.

Title: **Cover illustration/design**
Client: *X Funs*, Taiwanese Design Magazine

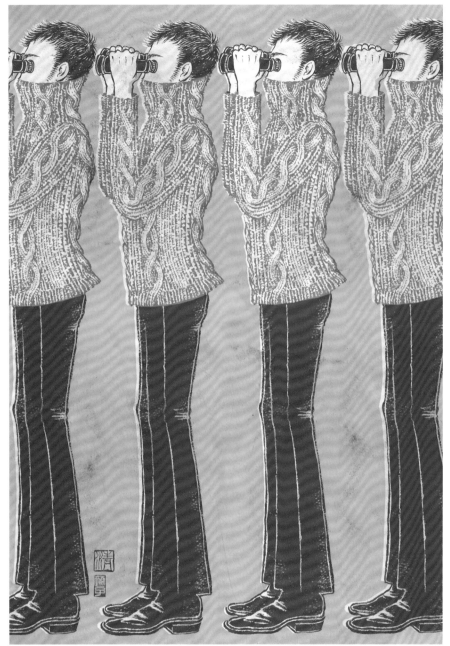

8 What's your icon in the artistic arena? What is the ultimate artist ideal to you?

Those who are "the originals," and/or those who aims to be one of them.

9 In what way do you think the illustration industry has changed? What do you think of the future trends in this industry?

I believe it is important to live "at present," and draw/paint like a person who lives "at present," but at the same time, I am doubtful of "trends." Trends come and go, and that is the reason why trends are called "trends."

Although, there are illustrators who chase trends, and they are popular, right at that moment. Because of that, I do not aim to be one of them.

I want to see things that transcend the "trends," or the kind of things that come and go quickly. I just want to be creating the kind of things that make me excited. At the end of the day, you want to be happy, don't you?

1   *2*

1
Title: **What Do We Sacrifice for Homeland Security?**
Client: Exhibition **EMBEDDED ART -Kunst im Namen**
                      der Sicherheit, Berlin
2
Title: **Gum package design**
Client: **Retail Advertising & Marketing Association,**
             Chicago

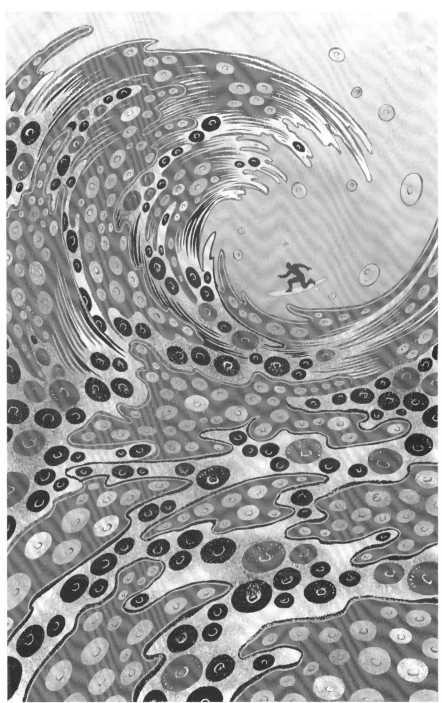

1 | 2 | 3

1-2
Title: Panel mural
Client: Robin Hood, PS96, Pentagram, Sagmeister Inc.
3
Title: Poster/banner created for individual exhibition
Client: Amarillo Centro de Dise in Xalapa, Mexico

1-2
Title: **Dunny**
Client: **Save the Children Foundation, New York**

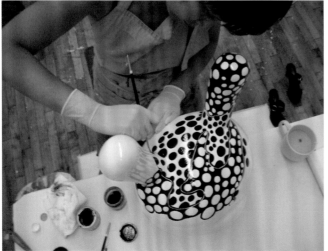

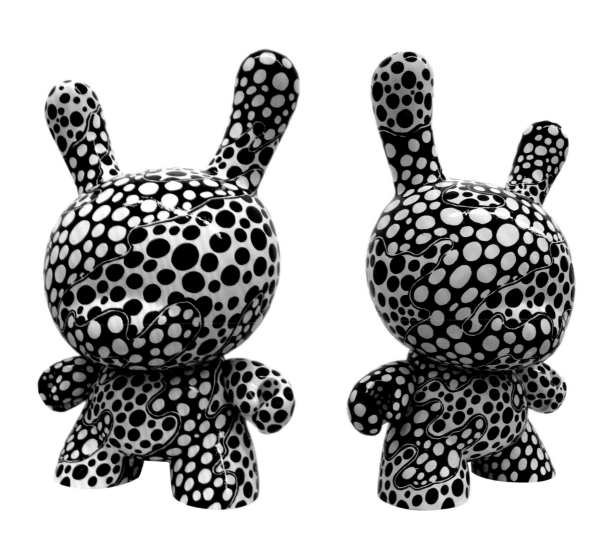

1 | 2

1-2
Title: **Four designs for T-shirts**
Client: **The GAP**

1

2   3   4

1
Title: **Tiger Beer ad campaign**
Client: **Tiger Beer, ad agency: CHI & Partners**
2
Title: **Monthly supplement CD cover**
Client: **The Word magazine of the UK**
3
Title: **Illustrations created for online advertising campaign/promotion**
Client: **Microsoft**
4
Title: **Limited edition diapers "Save the Tigers"**
Client: **Libero, ad agency: Forsman & Bodenfors**

(Cute baby photos are of Valdemar, son of graphic designer Truls Bärg
and photographer Charlotte Carlberg Bärg from Malmö, Sweden. Photo
copyrighted to Truls Bärg.)

BASE-V

Founded in Brazil's Sao Paulo by Danilo Oliveira, David Magila and Zansky, BASE-V has been actively cooperating with various media such as publication and graffiti. Out of unremitting exploration of materials and skills, the artists have established their core values, which has given rise to an evolutionary artist commucation means featuring collective creation based on respect for individuality. BASE-V is committed to presenting visual art to the public in a less detached manner in order to enhance its influence by making it more acceptable. Consequently, their illustrations exude a stronger sense of social responsibility for representing the voices of the contemporary and the public.

1 **When did you make up your mind to work as an illustrator? What happened then?**

It is very nice to us that the idea of mass culture and illustration are seen in many places at the same time. And it is a common way when you decide to begin doing this for a living.

2 **Please summarize your design concept. What has contributed to your current style?**

It is like a jazz band playing an improvisation. One of us can begin something on computer, on paper or on a wall, and the other guys come to do more until the artwork is finished. But of course, we would discuss the concept in advance. Our style is detailed, colorful, funny, aggressive and ironic.

3 **Where do you usually find the inspirations for your works? In other words, what do you usually do in the stage of design?**

Well, when we are doing a piece in a collaborative way, we will refer to a large quantity of works ranging from those of the masters to those of the youngest artists. I think this can contribute a little. But we are also influenced by the mass culture, pop culture, the people, the streets, and even dirty or violent elements.

4 **What do you think of the relationship between the artistic value and commercial value of the illustrations?**

We are watching a big wave of illustrators becoming artists in recent times. They are represented by galleries to sell their original works for a small fortune. It's very nice! But what can this really contribute for artistic thought? We love the illustrations that have uniqueness, both visually and conceptually. These kinds of works are between art and business. They can be considered art but were done specifically for a briefing, for a brand, for an editorial, etc. They are not for the purpose of discussing the limits of technique, concepts or ideas of the art.

5 **Have you found any conflict between drawing for your own fun and doing a commissioning work? How do you think the commercial operation has promoted this artistic creation?**

Of course this conflict exists. When you are drawing for yourself, you do what you want, while in commercial work, others tell you what to do.

6 **Nowadays, how can an illustrator be successful both in the artistic sense and the commercial sense? Do you have any experience to share with us?**

I'm sorry. I think we can come back to this question in the future.

7 **In what way do you think the illustration industry has changed? What do you think of the future trends in this industry?**

Here in Brazil illustrations are becoming more artistic than in the past. But we are far away from an ideal place for the artistic illustration. The hyper-realistic, realistic or non-authorial works are not prevalent yet. But we hope this can change as the global market begins to pay increasing attention to our creativity.

Title: **Book "Forests and Trees"**
Client: **El Bosque Editorial**
Illustrator: **Zansky**

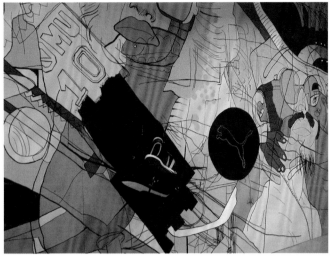

2	3	1
1	4	5
	6	7

1
Title: **Puma Clyde Poster**
Client: **Puma**
Illustrators: **Danilo Oliveira, David Magila, Rafael Coutinho and Zansky**
2-7
Title: **Puma Clyde wall painting installation**
Client: **Puma**
Illustrators: **Danilo Oliveira, David Magila, Rafael Coutinho and Zansky**

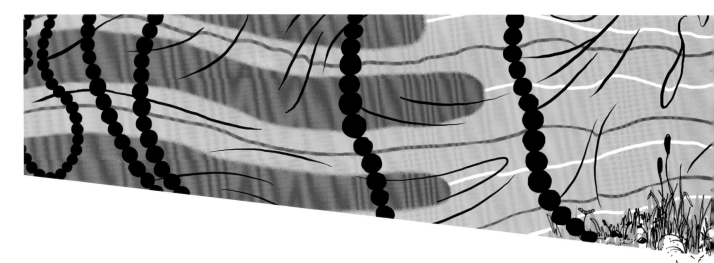

1
Title: **C&A Interprets Dior (layout for wall painting)**
Client: **C&A**
Illustrators: **Danilo Oliveira, David Magila and Zansky**
2-3
Title: **C&A Interprets Dior (Live painting in SPFW - Summer 2010)**
Client: **C&A**
Illustrators: **Danilo Oliveira, David Magila and Zansky**
4
Title: **C&A Interprets Dior**
Client: **C&A**
Illustrators: **Danilo Oliveira, David Magila and Zansky**

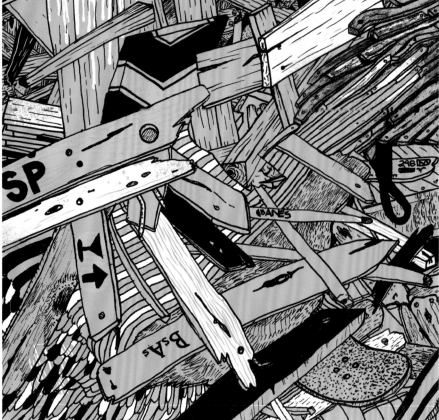

1
Title: BOX 2 (screen printing publication)
Client: BASE-V
Illustrators: Danilo Oliveira, David Magila, Rafael Coutinho and Zansky

2
Title: BOX 2 - Danilo Oliveira artwork (screen printing publication)
Client: BASE-V
Illustrator: Danilo Oliveira

3
Title: BOX 2 - Zansky artwork (screen printing publication)
Client: BASE-V
Illustrator: Zansky

4
Title: BOX 3 (screen printing publication)
Client: BASE-V
Illustrators: Danilo Oliveira, David Magila and Zansky

5
Title: BOX 3 cover (screen printing publication)
Client: BASE-V
Illustrators: Danilo Oliveira and David Magila

6
Title: All Kind (adhesive skin)
Client: Iskin Brasil
Illustrator: Zansky

1	3	4	5
2		6	

1
Title: **FFW Mag! #6 edition "Fire"**
Client: **FFWMag!**
Illustrators: **Danilo Oliveira and Zansky**
2
Title: **FFW Mag! #7 edition "Sao Paulo"**
Client: **FFWMag!**
Illustrators: **David Magila and Zansky**
3-5
Title: **Graphic #10 edition "Sketchbooks"**
Client: **Magma Books**
Illustrators: **Danilo Oliveira, David Magila, Rafael Coutinho and Zansky**
6
Title: **"Floating" (adhesive skin)**
Client: **Paste Skins**
Illustrator: **Zansky**

UNDOBOY

According to Undoboy, design breeds happiness. The artist from Malaysia always believes that the true meanings of design and illustration lie in spreading happiness. His illustration "Super Bastard" is a collection assembling boxes in a fashion of Rubik's Cube while incorporating illustration, giving many expressions to a single figure, creating happiness and interpreting human nature. Undoboy is also a successful advertising professional, whose clients include Nike, Coca Cola, Burger King, Volkswagen, Starbucks and so on. His works evidenced that an artist can be professional and artistically excellent at the same time, and manifested that design can bring happiness to others, as well as the artist himself.

1 When did you make up your mind to work as an illustrator? What happened then?

I started my career as a graphic designer. As a graphic designer, I always loved blending design with illustration. It turned out that illustration has become the main part of the story-telling in most of my works.

2 Please summarize your design concept. What has contributed to your current style?

I really enjoy creating design with interaction within it, because it gives more energy to the design. Therefore, I like working on designs that are more engaged with viewer emotions such as animation, interactive design, toy designs, and motion graphics. Design is fun and yet brings a lot of happiness to both the viewer and myself.

3 Where do you usually find the inspirations for your works? In other words, what do you usually do in the stage of design?

I enjoy being outside, because whatever I see, I will get inspired. A sign, a wild posting, a broken car, an old building, could lead me to imagine into other spaces. Music and movie are my inspirational sources too.

4 What do you think of the relationship between the artistic value and commercial value of the illustrations?

If they click together, the chemistry will work and it will generate a great result. If not, it will turn out badly.

5 Have you found any conflict between drawing for your own fun and doing a commissioning work? How do you think the commercial operation has promoted this artistic creation?

Works for commercial projects is very different from the work I'm doing on my own. However, most of the people asking me to do illustration because they like looking at my illustration style. So, I end up making something that I enjoy even though I'm doing it for a commercial project.

6 Nowadays, how can an illustrator be successful both in the artistic sense and the commercial sense? Do you have any experience to share with us?

A commercial job is never that satisfying. I'm still learning to utilize my creative juice on commercial projects. The process is not easy as sometimes I have found a lot of disagreements between my point of view and the client's perspective. Those projects that work out great usually have a good balance between both being creative and good marketing.

7 As an illustrator, how do you interpret the role you are playing?

Be optimistic and work on something that I like.

8 What's your icon in the artistic arena? What is the ultimate artist ideal to you?

Works by the artist Takashi Murakami have had a very strong impact on my beliefs. Illustrations and toys by Michael Lau, Yoshitomo Nara, Yuko Shimizu, Chris Ware, James Jarvis, Kaws and Jamie Hewlett are fascinating.

9 In what way do you think the illustration industry has changed? What do you think of the future trends in this industry?

There will be more crossovers between cultures. Art is going to be borderless.

Title: **Boxie Family**
Client: **Undoboy**

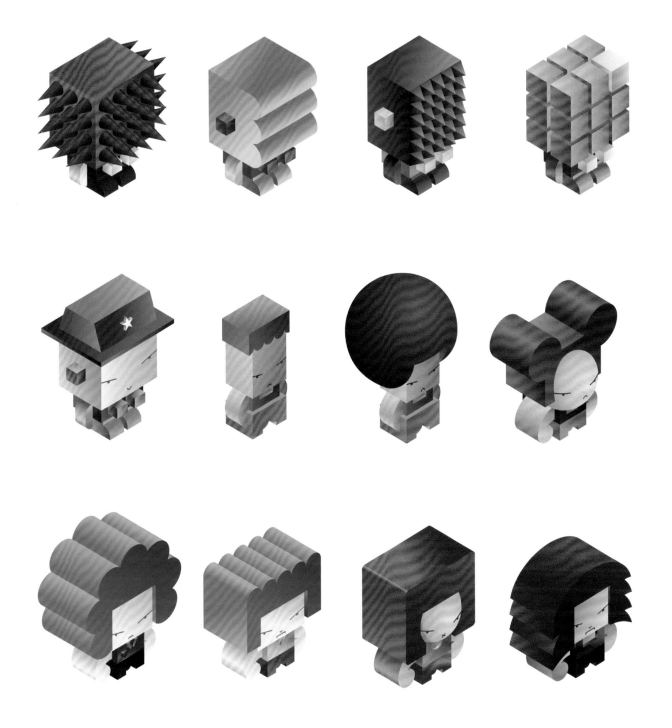

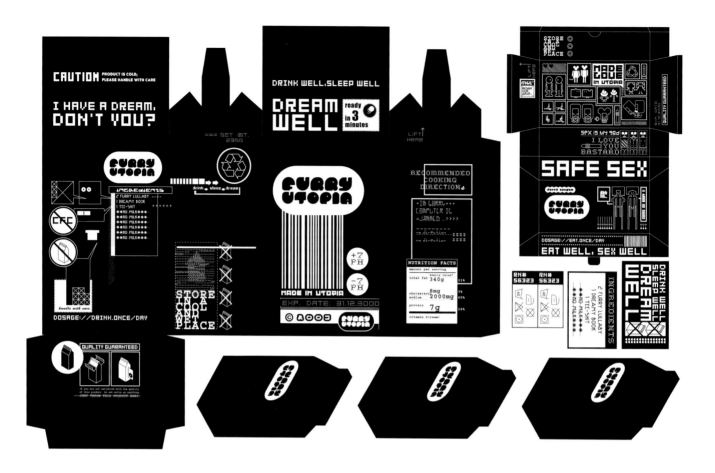

```
1   3     6
2   4   5
```

1
Title: Happy Holiday
Client: Undoboy Online Store
2
Title: Grand Opening
Client: Undoboy Online Store
3
Title: Ping Pong Remix
Client: Gaston Caba

4
Title: Clone
Client: Sciencewerk.com
5
Title: Design Propanganda
Client: Foreign Policy Design Group
6
Title: Amoda
Client: Amoda

1-2
Title: **Little Undo**
Client: **Undoboy**
3
Title: **Characteristic Icons**
Client: **Undoboy**

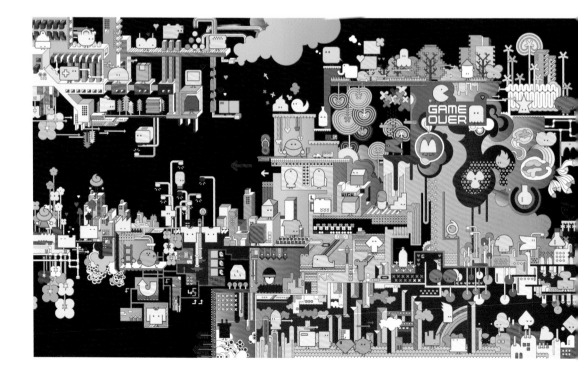

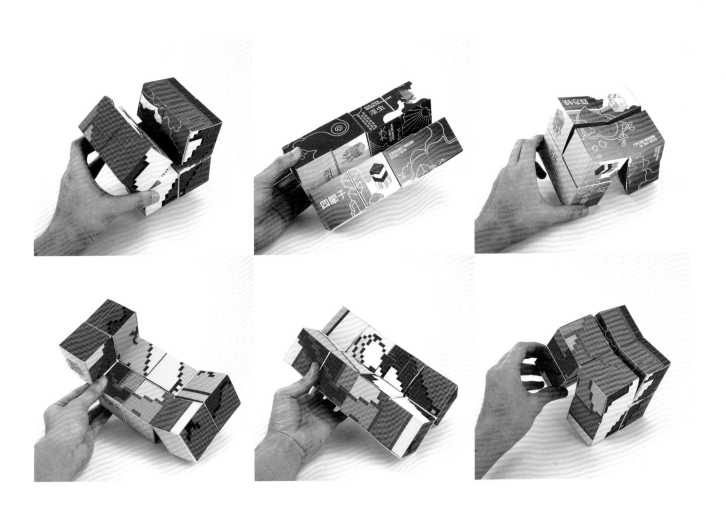

1 2 | 4
  3 |

1-2
Title: Wall Decal
Client: Blik
3-4
Title: Super-Bastard Box Art
Client: Undoboy

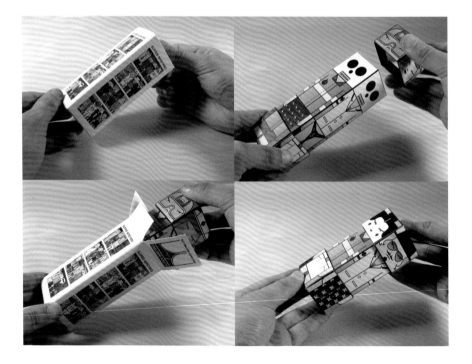

WONABC

This avant-garde illustrator from Bayern in Germany is passionate about exploration of Gothic style, religion and death. However, this does not mean that his works are anchored to negative elements. On the contrary, his works are defined by bright and delicate color, complicated and massive structure, permeating with a typical German precision. These illustrations are visually powerful and pleasing. Representing the illustrators sticking to a less traveled path, Wonabc is inspired by street arts, opposing to restraints and science and celebrating freedom and human nature.

1 **When did you make up your mind to work as an illustrator? What happened then?**

Normally I work as a free artist, illustration jobs happen by accident.

2 **Please summarize your design concept. What has contributed to your current style?**

Supposedly the essence of painting and creating is not to become stiff in your expression. Shape and form are tools with which to work, they should never be self-explanatory. The form, shape and direction are just a medium for life's elixir, to make the essence of life artistically visual in total harmony with body and soul. Everyday I have to break the mould. Everyday I have to renew myself similar to life itself in the continual river of change. Human chameleon style. Every set form as mighty as it may be conceals the path towards truth. Life knows no boundaries. Chaos rules this place where we dwell.

3 **Where do you usually find the inspirations for your works? In other words, what do you usually do in the stage of design?**

By life itself, a lot by travelling the world.

4 **What do you think of the relationship between the artistic value and commercial value of the illustrations?**

I do not care, I only do jobs in which I can do what I want.

5 **Have you found any conflict between drawing for your own fun and doing a commissioning work? How do you think the commercial operation has promoted this artistic creation?**

No, there is no conflict for me. I always do my best.

6 **Nowadays, how can an illustrator be successful both in the artistic sense and the commercial sense? Do you have any experience to share with us?**

Normally I earn my money by selling my free art. I try only to do commercial jobs in which I could also sell projects similar to my free art.

7 **As an illustrator, how do you interpret the role you are playing?**

Visual entertainment.

8 **What's your icon in the artistic arena? What is the ultimate artist ideal to you?**

It is probably the most beautiful way to change this wonderfully shitty world with your art pieces by creating a contra world. Something that reduces the hyper-mighty negative energies of this world. I build a new world, a world full of color.

9 **In what way do you think the illustration industry has changed? What do you think of the future trends in this industry?**

I would like that illustration would get more place in the printing industries like it did in the 19th and 20th century. Companies should not always only look to their financial benefit. The industry should be reminded that by their money power they have a responsibility for visual health and the culture for this planet. By globalization the real big industry leaders are more powerful than any king in human history.

Title: Panda Camou Cloudz
Client: Carhartt Europe Spring Summer 2007 Print Campain

1
Title: Buffalo Soldier
Client: Carhartt Europe Spring Summer 2007 Print Campain
2
Title: Kroko vs C
Client: Carhartt Europe Spring Summer 2007 Print Campain

1 2 3

1
Title: **Emu Case**
Client: **Carhartt Europe Spring Summer 2007 Print Campain**
2
Title: **Kitty Red Stripe**
Client: **Carhartt Europe Spring Summer 2007 Print Campain**
3
Title: **Creatish Octopus**
Client: **Carhartt Europe Spring Summer 2007 Print Campain**

AKINORI
OISHI

Simpler things tend to be more appealing. Akinori Oishi's works are reminiscent of graffiti master Keith Haring. Both artists have marveled the world with the simplest lines. Warm-hearted and well-connected, Akinori always creates graffiti for her friends' exhibitions and shows, which are often well-received. Active in installation and animation, Akinori employs lines that smile to you. Her works are comparted to art amusement part brimming over happiness and liveliness through repetitive use of smiling expressions, and creative application of games, space and installation arts.

1 When did you make up your mind to work as an illustrator? What happened then?

I don't know when exactly. I just love drawing since I was a little kid, and now here I am an artist or illustrator.

2 Please summarize your design concept. What has contributed to your current style?

My style is a kind of pictogram illustration, or I should say it's a pattern universe of my drawing style. I prefer to draw minimal and abstract expressions.

3 Where do you usually find the inspirations for your works? In other words, what do you usually do in the stage of design?

I go to the library once a week; then I read series of books about geography all over the world. And I feel like traveling. It's enjoyable to look at photos from many areas, Asia, Europe, U.S., Latin America and Africa etc.... I think that is my inspiration.

4 What do you think of the relationship between the artistic value and commercial value of the illustrations?

The first one — artistic — is for me, and the second one — commercial — is for you.

5 Have you found any conflict between drawing for your own fun and doing a commissioning work? How do you think the commercial operation has promoted this artistic creation?

If one client asked me for something quite commercial, it would be difficult. But I will try and discuss with the client to find a good way to show my style as much as possible.

6 Nowadays, how can an illustrator be successful both in the artistic sense and the commercial sense? Do you have any experience to share with us?

If the illustrator finds his or her best style, which is the most unique design ever in the world, the success comes on both the artistic and the commercial sense eventually. I just believe it!

7 As an illustrator, how do you interpret the role you are playing?

I am playing on paper in a flat universe.

8 What's your icon in the artistic arena? What is the ultimate artist ideal to you?

Drawaholic, it is what I call myself — the handmade copy and paste function to fill all the paper with my multiple characters. It is a kind of crazy job in fact! But it's interesting to do it by myself because nobody else is doing it.

9 In what way do you think the illustration industry has changed? What do you think of the future trends in this industry?

The interactive graphics!

Title: **Golden Potatoes**
Client: **Pictopia / Pictoplasma (Germany)**

1-5
Title: **Very Fun Park**
Client: **Fubon Art Foundation**

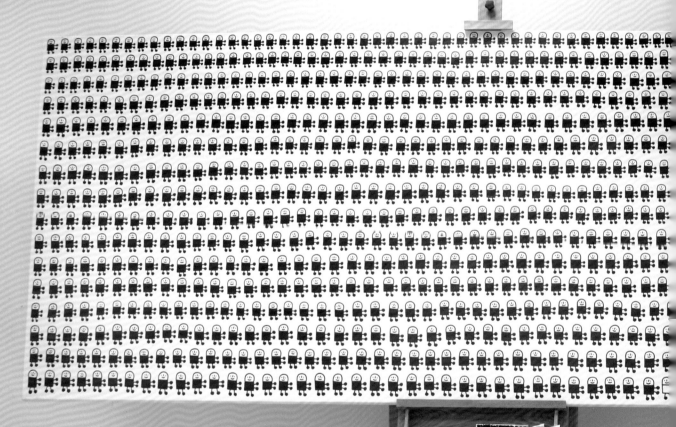

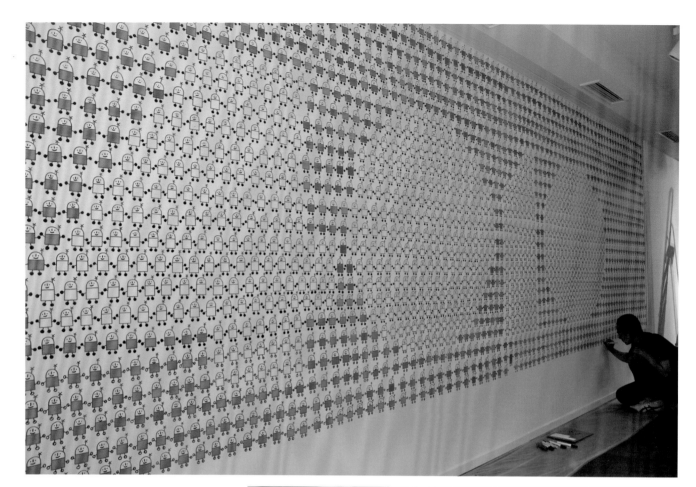

1 | 4
  3 | 5
2 | 6

1-2
Title: **4010**
Client: **Deutsche Telekom (Germany)**
3-6
Title: Pencils
Client: **Illustrative (Germany)**

1	2		5
	3		
	4	6	7

1
Title: **Bugs**
Client: **Yo Gabba / Nickelodeon (USA)**
2-3
Title: **Happy Living**
Client: **Museum of Tomorrow**
4
Title: **Talking Boxes**
Client: **Pictoplasma (Germany)**
5
Title: **Pillow**
Client: **Eugene & Pauline (France)**
6
Title: **Baby Pants**
Client: **Self-Production (Japan)**
7
Title: **Baby TV**
Client: **Makoo (Japan)**

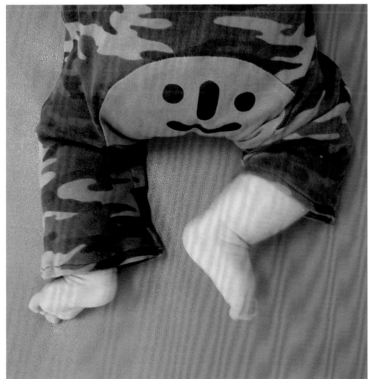

JON BURGERMAN

As one of the most active illustration artists in the UK, Jon Burgerman is recognized by the public mainly due to his seeminly random and intuitve shapes, interweavig lines and stimulating passions. He has established his name in this industry with works flowing with rich color and vigor. His multi-dimensional style incorporates a contemporary trademark featuring optimism, while inspired by typical English self-mockery, naive passion, and intrinsic humor. He has been engaged in many areas, including illustration, painting, printed products, animation, massive graffiti and product design.

1 When did you make up your mind to work as an illustrator? What happened then?

I didn't ever make up my mind. I was a Fine Art graduate and was offered some work that involved making a painting for an album cover, without knowing it that was my first illustration job. To me I was just making an image and never thought of it as illustration.

2 Please summarize your design concept. What has contributed to your current style?

I like to have lines with rhythm and colors that are musical and compliment each other, even in discord.

3 Where do you usually find the inspirations for your works? In other words, what do you usually do in the stage of design?

I don't really think I would go looking for inspiration, I just try and read, look at and experience different things, and without knowing I can become inspired.

4 What do you think of the relationship between the artistic value and commercial value of the illustrations?

This is a very open question. These values can change over time. I do not have a good answer for it, to be honest. At one point in time someone is asked to design a logo or an illustration for something, say a film poster; then fifty years later the same design is shown in a museum and everyone calls it a work of art.

5 Have you found any conflict between drawing for your own fun and doing a commissioning work? How do you think the commercial operation has promoted this artistic creation?

I think my personal work has paved the way for commercial projects. I am very lucky that for most commercial projects I have free control to create what I like. I always try to avoid a distinction between being commercial and demonstrating personal styles, I just try and satisfy my own ambitions and aspirations.

6 Nowadays, how can an illustrator be successful both in the artistic sense and the commercial sense? Do you have any experience to share with us?

I think either way you have to be an artist. Have your own thoughts and beliefs in how to create and why you make in this way. Then try and apply these to whatever project you are working on. Success can mean many things. I think the best kind of success allows you to be proud of your work and to sleep well at night.

7 As an illustrator, how do you interpret the role you are playing?

Hmm.... I'm not sure I understand what you are asking? My role, in my mind, is to make works that are interesting to me and hopefully to others.

8 What's your icon in the artistic arena? What is the ultimate artist ideal to you?

I'm not sure I have an icon. There are lots of interesting artists and I guess as you are asking about commercial works and personal works. I think works from people like Warhol and the Pop Artists are quite interesting to look at.

9 In what way do you think the illustration industry has changed? What do you think of the future trends in this industry?

Illustration means so many things now. It may refer to illustration but also design and art and motion and conceptual toying. Illustration is a little bit of many visual practices now. In the future this will only continue to happen.

Title: **Lungerful print**
Client: **American Cancer Society**

1	2	3	
4	5	7	8
	6		

1-3
Title: Sony Home apparel
Client: Lockwood / Sony Home
4-5
Title: USB Memory Card
Client: *Computer Arts* Magazine
6
Title: The Letter J
Client: Made In Birmingham
7
Title: Lossy Botany Lab
Client: Jon Burgerman / Heliumcowboy
8
Title: Cats
Client: burgerplex.com

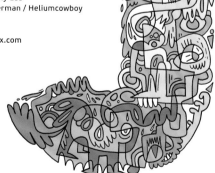

NICHOLAS
DI GENOVA

Born in 1981, Nicolas Di
Genova is based in Toronto, Canada.
His illustrations represent a special integration
of realism and surrealism in terms of living forms
and geometric shapes. Just as he remarks, "they are all
tightly controlled by order, like shrouded in a formal suit that
does not fit, tidy, mechanical but embrassed." He is passionate
about depicting species evolution, and re-constructing a brand-
new life order by confusing the logics. He rejects the idea of
using bright colors, leaving his works enveloped in coldness
and absurdity, meanwhile demonstrating a scientific
precision. Nocholas Di Genova often works with galleries
rather than cooperating with brands.

Photographer : **Brittany Shepherd**

1 **When did you make up your mind to work as an illustrator? What happened then?**

When I was a kid I knew that I wanted to either draw for a living, or become a zoologist. I ended up taking the middle ground, I suppose. I just started drawing all the time when I was about five; it was the natural thing for me to do, and I never stopped. Now I still draw all the time, but I've managed to turn it into the sort of thing that I can live off.

2 **Please summarize your design concept. What has contributed to your current style?**

My design concept is based around the idea of utilizing the various allegorical meanings that have been attributed to various animals, to create chimeras. These chimeras are my way of speaking to the audience, to express my world view in a way. The biggest influences on my style have been my life-long obsession with traditional natural science illustration, and my teenage obsession with anime and manga.

3 **Where do you usually find the inspirations for your works? In other words, what do you usually do in the stage of design?**

In other words, what do you usually do in the stage of design? Leading up to a new drawing, I usually go through all my old sketchbooks to find a random note or idea that I jotted down along the way. An example of this is the drawing I'm working on now, about a type of fungus (cordyceps), that generally infects and alters the behavior of invertebrates, making them act in a way that they would not before the infection. I thought it would be interesting to illustrate a type of mind-controlling fungus that could infect vertebrates. So I have the initial idea, then I spend a lot of time reading up on subjects that could inform that idea (in this case, various types of fungus and texts on possession and exorcisms), then I start laying out the piece, and go from there...

4 **What do you think of the relationship between the artistic value and commercial value of the illustrations?**

I think each case would have to be judged separately.... a lot of work with commercial value can still have a lot of artistic merit, if you are pushing yourself to try new things and pushing the limits of your skills. However, a lot of illustrators just continue to do the same old thing because they know it will sell, and although that's part of making a living, that sort of work behavior has little artistic merit.

5 **Have you found any conflict between drawing for your own fun and doing a commissioning work? How do you think the commercial operation has promoted this artistic creation?**

Most of my work is made for a gallery setting, that's just where I'm comfortable.

6 **Nowadays, how can an illustrator be successful both in the artistic sense and the commercial sense? Do you have any experience to share with us?**

I don't have very much personal experience; but yes, of course. Look at all those people who are showing in LA with an illustrative style, the "Juxtapoz Artists" I guess they're called. Many of them have artistic careers just as strong as their illustration careers. It's an interesting time to be an illustrator I think.

7 **As an illustrator, how do you interpret the role you are playing?**

I don't play any role as an illustrator, but as an artist my role is clear: I draw the stuff I'm into. It sounds overly simplistic, but it is the most concise way of explaining what I do.

8 **What's your icon in the artistic arena? What is the ultimate artist ideal to you?**

To continue to absorb information, process it in my mind, and to draw my reaction to it. And to spend the majority of every day of my life doing this. That is the ultimate artist ideal to me.

Title: **Zebrasaur**

9 In what way do you think the illustration industry has changed? What do you think of the future trends in this industry?

Again, I'm not very familiar with the history or the present state of the illustration industry. But the art industry has opened up in a way lately that favors illustrators. In the last 10 years, maybe because of the success of artists like Takashi Murakami, Jeff Soto, and David Choe, the artistic institution has opened up to people with more illustrative styles in a way unlike before, which benefits both illustrators and artists in my opinion. The down side is that a lot of young artists and illustrators see this, and think that the path to success is to emulate these people exactly. For every Jeff Soto there are one hundred people emulating, and these just waters down the "movement." This type of emulation really needs to stop....

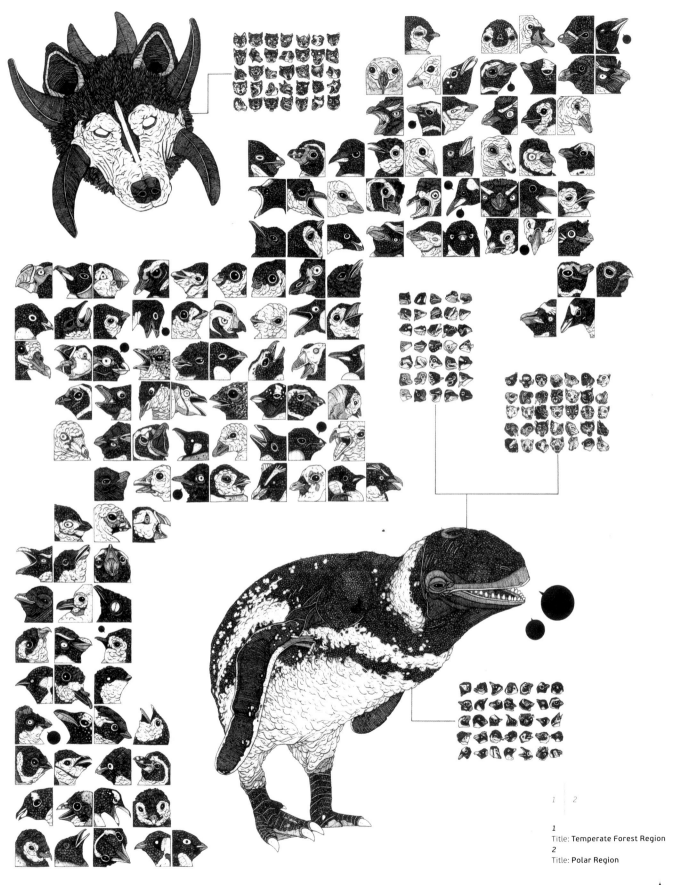

1
Title: **Temperate Forest Region**
2
Title: **Polar Region**

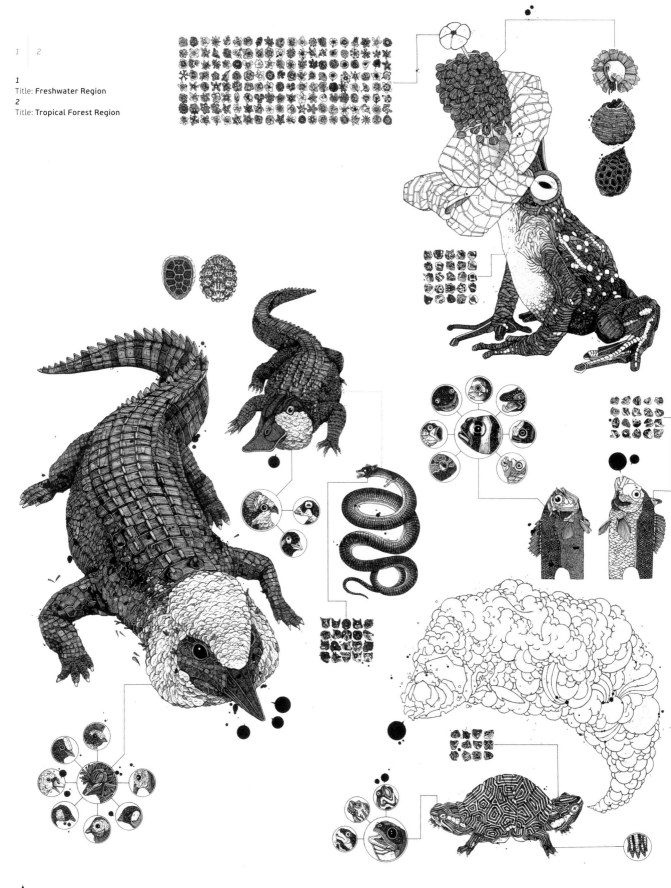

1   2

1
Title: Freshwater Region
2
Title: Tropical Forest Region

1
Title: **Desert Region**
2
Title: **Marine Region**

NICHOLAS DI GENOVA 09

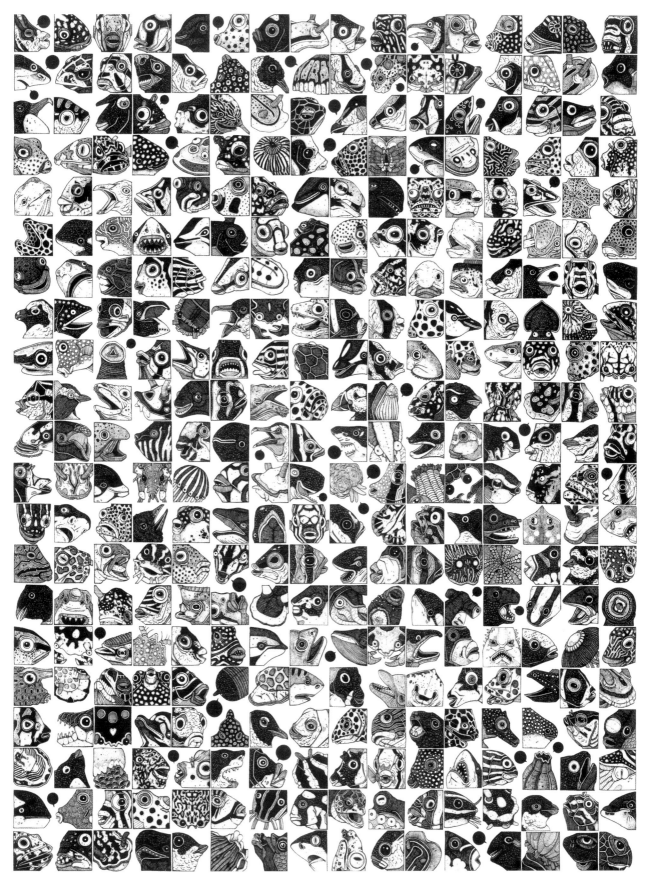

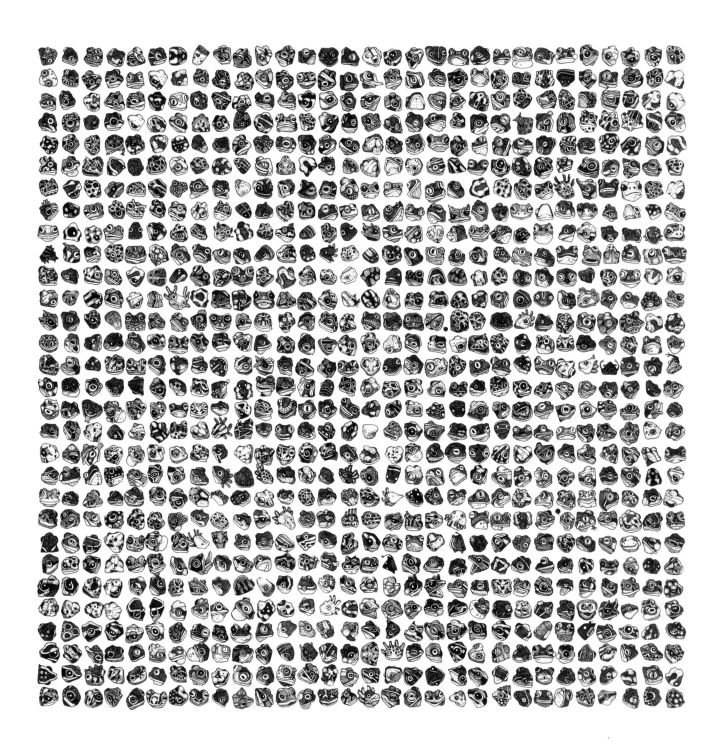

1-2
Title: **900 Amphibians**

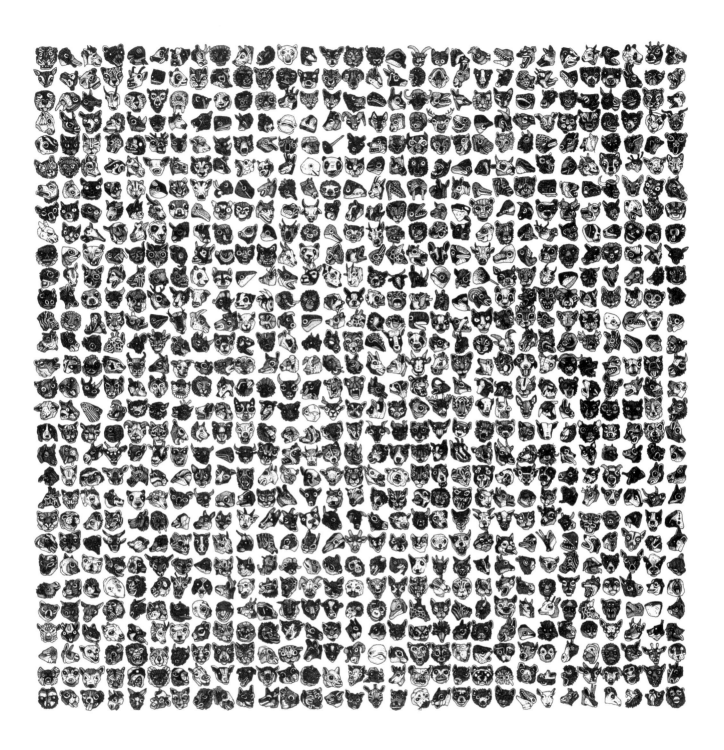

STÉPHANE BLANQUET

Born in France, Stéphane Blanquet is immune to the ordinary and popular, preferring absurd and bizzarre images. His works are highly recognizable and strongly striking. Even though the audience might be resistant to something absurd and creepy in his works, one cannot deny the breathing, wild, and magical alluring power they exude. This power seems to be unreal, but Stéphane Blanquet can still feel its existence, because "what is visible to me is indeed uncommon," according to Blanquet. He lives true to his title "ghost's painter."

1 When did you make up your mind to work as an illustrator? What happened then?

I have drawn since decades ago, and I did not have the chance to publish until fifteen years old. I started to publish works regularly in newspapers twenty years ago.

2 Please summarize your design concept. What has contributed to your current style?

I like shattering the world. I enjoy working on various media, such as theater, illustration, installation, video....I like the diversity. I like art in 3D.

3 Where do you usually find the inspirations for your works? In other words, what do you usually do in the stage of design?

The original inspiration comes from the desire to make fun. I like artists like Roland Topor, who are brilliant in playing with arts and know about all the media. And of course I like drawing my dream, my fantasy, and the unreal world.

4 What do you think of the relationship between the artistic value and commercial value of the illustrations?

This is an interesting question. There is always fun with the constraint. The constraint is important. I have now learnt to focus on the freedom.

5 Have you found any conflict between drawing for your own fun and doing a commissioning work? How do you think the commercial operation has promoted this artistic creation?

Of course I see things differently. People often ask me to draw my universe. For example, I did condom wrappings because my world is sexual. They call me because I have a special universe, so the commercials ask me for specials things, monster, strange case, etc....

6 Nowadays, how can an illustrator be successful both in the artistic sense and the commercial sense? Do you have any experience to share with us?

I would like not to become too accessible. I like it when the reader can't tell the difference between a commercial project and my universe. I like to see my theatrical posters in the streets. I like it when my images are in the streets; it's better than in a museum. I love Keith Haring's work for this reason.

7 As an illustrator, how do you interpret the role you are playing?

I work a lot for the theater and see how the audience will react to my work, especially the audience who knows nothing about me before....I like the pictures, as well as the way the universe moves.

My role is to provoke reactions, whether positive or negative.

8 What's your icon in the artistic arena? What is the ultimate artist ideal to you?

I love it when the universe changes, or the singular becomes classic. My favorite artists include Gary Panter and Topor.

9 In what way do you think the illustration industry has changed? What do you think of the future trends in this industry?

Many artists who were originally not interested in illustration have started to engage in this industry. I'd like to see more things which will become even more bizarre and personal.

Title: **Diorama**
Client: **la Comédie de Caen**

1
Title: Packaging of condom
Client: la Comédie de Caen
2-3
Title: Photographies of SADE SONGS
Client: SADE SONGS
4-7
Title: Toys in Wood

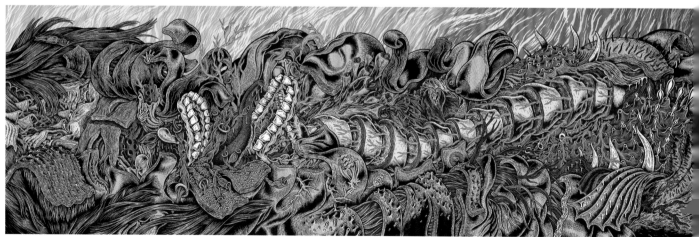

1
Title: Illustration for NONSTOP
Client: NONSTOP
2
Title: DIORAMA
Client: le comédie de Caen
3-4
Title: Illsustration for disc book for Mami Chan
Client: Mami Chan

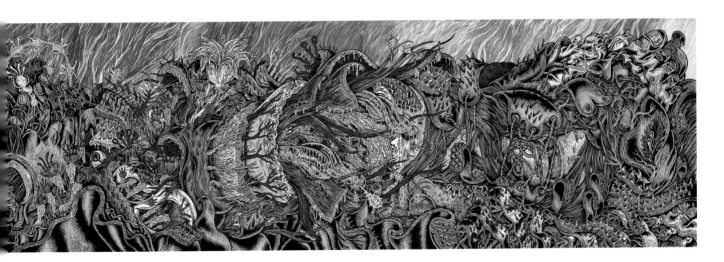

1
Title: Illsutration for BLAB!
Client: BLAB!
2
Title: Illustration for Sortez la chienne
Client: Sortez la chienne
3
Title: Body painting
Client: la bandaison
4
Title: Betty Hairy Honey toys
Client: Lulu Japan
5
Title: Body paitning on a Japanese girl

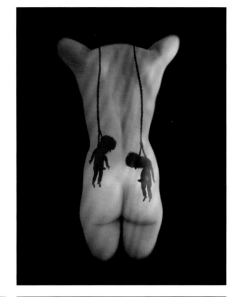

KEIICHI TANAAMI

Having pioneered the avant-garde and pop arts in the 1960s, Keiichi Tanaami is a Japanese visual artist. He served as the first art director of the Japanese edition of *Playboy*, as well as fashion designer and industrial product designer. It is quite easy to identify his works, which are defined by visual images of strong color and rich information, clipping creation, in addtion to absurd and mysterious visual symbols. His inspirations are rooted in imagination and dreams, incorporating pop and traditionally oriental pictorial elements. He is recognized as one of the key figures in Japanese contemorary visual design industry.

1 **When did you make up your mind to work as an illustrator? What happened then?**

When I was a child, we had "E-mono-gatari", a popular genre of storybooks with illustration in Japan. I think my strong yearning to Soji Yamakawa, one of the most popular "E-mono-gatari" artists, led me to this world.

2 **Please summarize your design concept. What has contributed to your current style?**

Uniqueness and originality, which doesn't have parallel elsewhere.

3 **Where do you usually find the inspirations for your works? In other words, what do you usually do in the stage of design?**

I get inspiration from everything around me. Film, literature, music, traveling, eating and taking a walk, the list goes on forever. Taking a walk in the morning especially excites my brain, and sets off new images.

4 **What do you think of the relationship between the artistic value and commercial value of the illustrations?**

I work without any demur to the field of illustration, so I take offers up when they accept all of my creation. I accept offers if they need my art.

5 **Have you found any conflict between drawing for your own fun and doing a commissioning work? How do you think the commercial operation has promoted this artistic creation?**

I don't distinguish between my painting works and illustration, because people who offer me work understand my creation, so I can work with 100 percent of my thoughts.

6 **Nowadays, how can an illustrator be successful both in the artistic sense and the commercial sense? Do you have any experience to share with us?**

If people want to create work of good quality, never think of easy concessions.

7 **What's your icon in the artistic arena? What is the ultimate artist ideal to you?**

The artist, who influenced me most, is Kyosai Kawanabe, a Japanese artist in the Edo era called "the bizarre artist." All of his works give me strong vibes still today.

8 **In what way do you think the illustration industry has changed? What do you think of the future trends in this industry?**

I don't know.

Title: **Red-colored Bridge**

1-4
Client: *Wallpaper* magazine

EESHAUN

Born in the 1980s, Eeshaun has never received formal education in painting. As a lucky bird, he has attracted wide attention since commissioned by Adidas and become an established figure in the illustration industry. His works are contemporary and light-hearted, clear-cut and simple. Passionate about Akira Toriyama's anime, he was so obsessed with the vivid color and funny characters in it that he kept scribbling every day, without missing any details. Eeshaun still works as a teacher in a college in Singapore, committed to assisting the students to evolve into rising artists. According to him, on the way to become a successful illustrator, it does not matter what you are and how talented you are. The true answer lies in passion.

1 **When did you make up your mind to work as an illustrator? What happened then?**

Actually I didn't! I was just drawing and putting my work on my website (gardensilly.com) back in 2005. Suddenly people started asking me to draw for them, and one thing led to another.

2 **Please summarize your design concept. What has contributed to your current style?**

Hmm....I always think it was a sort of natural style I had — but on a deeper level, it was probably a personal response to the grey, built-up environment around me. I was opposed to planning and sketching my work, so the organic style developed out of improvisation and experimentation. Also I enjoy colorful things, which explains why I like using bright and loud colors in my work whenever I can. There isn't much of a concept for the drawings; I like to make up narratives and characters as I go along.

3 **Where do you usually find the inspirations for your works? In other words, what do you usually do in the stage of design?**

I find inspiration from other artists who have similar styles or aesthetics — usually colorful, whimsical and abstract art appeals to me. But if I don't get inspired, I'll just draw until something fun appears on the paper.

4 **What do you think of the relationship between the artistic value and commercial value of the illustrations?**

It's getting increasingly common for artists and illustrators to be able to express themselves through more adventurous clients who're looking for something different, usually through a distinctive aesthetic or artistic interpretation of their product; so it is possible for art and commerce to meet without much sacrifice.

5 **Have you found any conflict between drawing for your own fun and doing a commissioning work? How do you think the commercial operation has promoted this artistic creation?**

Hmm hardly, I think I've been lucky to get clients who engage me for my drawings - so I haven't had to make much sacrifice in terms of artistic creation or integrity. Commercial application is important in giving the artist recognition, and sometimes it also gives the work a broader or stronger market appeal.

6 **Nowadays, how can an illustrator be successful both in the artistic sense and the commercial sense? Do you have any experience to share with us?**

I think one way is to stick to a distinctive style or look — so people recognize you for it. It might be tough at the beginning, but you'll get clients once you've created that brand or identity around your work it — becomes an association with your name. Also it pays to do some free work if the job is interesting and lets you explore different products or mediums, so people understand the full potential of your artistic creation.

7 **As an illustrator, how do you interpret the role you are playing?**

I always see illustration as a support role to graphic design; it also serves as a means of image-making. Illustration is powerful because it can alter the visual landscape and feeling of our environment, and possibly ignite the imagination of the public.

8 **What's your icon in the artistic arena? What is the ultimate artist ideal to you?**

My icon is the character with the smiling, sleepy face. In a high-strung society where everyone is working intensely for money and deadlines, I think the face helps them relax and laugh a little. The ultimate artist ideal is to be able to achieve what you want and express it exactly as how you saw it in your mind.

Title: **Hyperheadache**
Client: **Hypercolor Exhibition@Loft**

9 In what way do you think the illustration industry has changed? What do you think of the future trends in this industry?

The influence of software has given rise to many "digital" looking illustrations. The future depends on what new technology surfaces and how people use it to their advantage. I also expect illustrators to respond to technological tools by continuously going backwards to tradition, i.e. through print making, or by juxtaposing and fusing digital tools with traditional styles of image-making.

1 | 4 5
2 3 | 6

1-5
Title: **T3CHNO Ravers & Guerrilla Gardeners installation**
Client: **Adidas (Adiartist Exhibition)**
6
Title: **Chaos in the Disco (Acrylic on wood panel)**
Client: **Adidas (Adiartist Exhibition)**

```
1  2    8
3  4  5
     6    9
     7
```

1-7
Title: **Original Creatures!**
Client: Adidas (Adidas 60th Anniversary House Party)
8
Title: **Youth Olympic Games Mural**
Client: Singapore Youth Olympic Games Committee
9
Title: **Singapore Supergarden, 11th Venice Biennale**
Client: **Design Singapore Council**

1		4
2		5
3		

1-3
Title: Anything Also Anyhow
Client: ActuallyActually boutique

4
Title: Little Misty Mural
Client: PATH market

5
Title: Bubbly-Gumley!
Client: ION Orchard, Singapore

1-6
Title: **MOVE! Bishan Circle Line**
   (Art-in-Transit) murals
Client: **Land Transport Authority, Singapore**

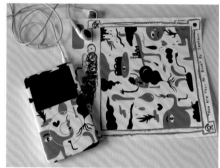

1 2 | 3

1
Title: **Ellie Blue & Friends**
Client: **Zookimono (France)**
2
Title: **Multiple Purplexities**
Client: **Fabrix**
3
Title: **Alvar Aalto Iittala**
Client: **Style Nordic**

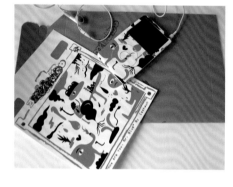
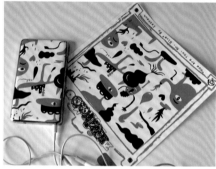

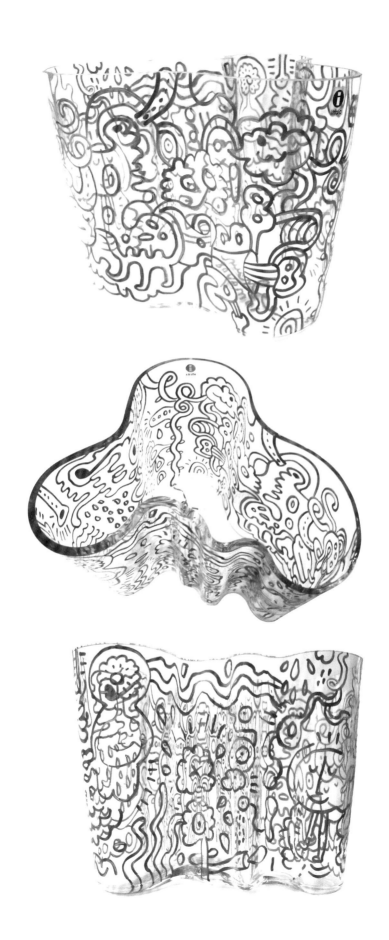

LORENZO PETRANTONI

Born in Genoa, Lorenzo Petrantoni is inspired by the late seventeenth century. In his spare time, he clips the illustrations in outdated newspaper and magainzes and rummaged in ancient French dictionary for inspiration, striving to regenerate the aged images. He gives the clips a particular beauty of order in a rigorous manner. He arranges shapes in a logical way but not rigid way. He is frequently commissioned by editorial and journal giants due to outstanding quality, ordered beauty and restrained delight in his works, which make active presence in various mainstream media.

1 When did you make up your mind to work as an illustrator? What happened then?

It was all by chance. I never imagined becoming an illustrator. I have always been the art director in advertising agencies.

2 Please summarize your design concept. What has contributed to your current style?

The design is the search for beauty. My style was born of two passions, history and graphics.

3 Where do you usually find the inspirations for your works? In other words, what do you usually do in the stage of design?

All the work comes from the illustrations that I find in old books.

4 What do you think of the relationship between the artistic value and commercial value of the illustrations?

The two values live together. There is no value if there is no quality.

5 Have you found any conflict between drawing for your own fun and doing a commissioning work? How do you think the commercial operation has promoted this artistic creation?

The commercial part is important. Without it, work would not exist. There are wonderful works that remain locked in dusty closets that have been are already forgotten.

6 Nowadays, how can an illustrator be successful both in the artistic sense and the commercial sense? Do you have any experience to share with us?

I think the commercial part is very important. Many works that I have sold were intended as works of art.

7 What's your icon in the artistic arena? What is the ultimate artist ideal to you?

I really like the paintings of Diego Rivera and Frida Kalo.

8 In what way do you think the illustration industry has changed? What do you think of the future trends in this industry?

I think that the picture will evolve into art. The need is to find new languages, and new interpretations.

Title: **Amsterdam**
Client: **Moooi Design**

THE 37th ANNUAL GUIDE TO THE BEST OF EVERYTHING
328 WINNERS!

Boston

FUN

SERVICES

THE BEST OF BOSTON 2010

FOOD

SHOPPING ET STYLE

1
Title: Cover design
Client: *Boston* Magazine
2
Title: Cover design
Client: Family Circle
3
Title: Cover design
Client: *Billboard* Magazine
4
Title: Personal Invitation

1
Title: Cover design
Client: Time Out New York
2
Title: Illustration for a poet

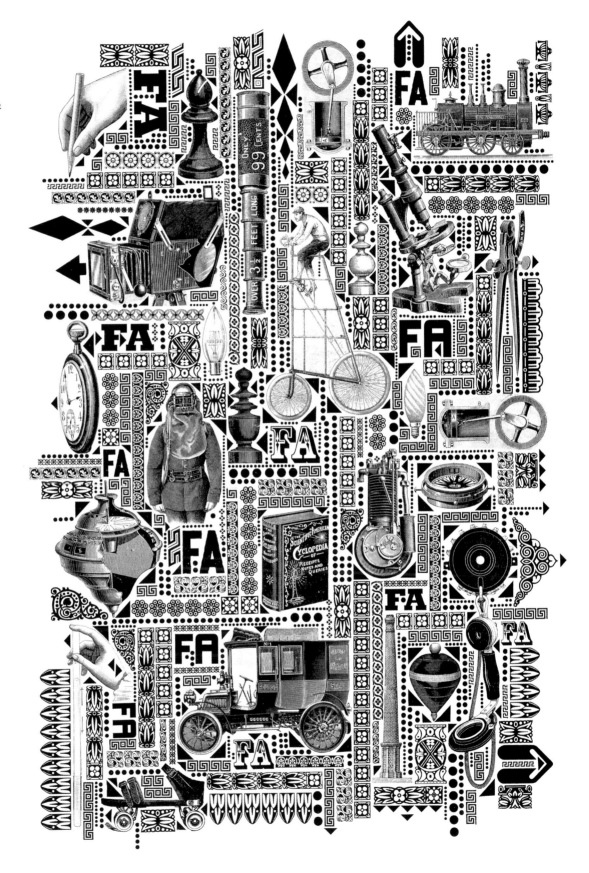

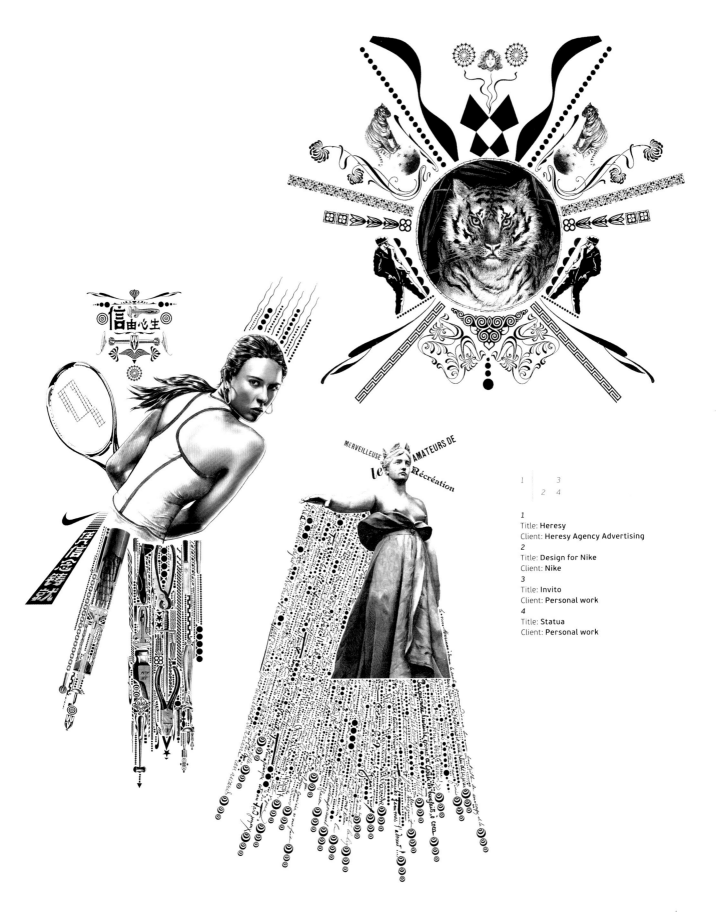

1 | | 3
| 2 | 4

1
Title: Heresy
Client: Heresy Agency Advertising
2
Title: Design for Nike
Client: Nike
3
Title: Invito
Client: Personal work
4
Title: Statua
Client: Personal work

ALEXANDER GORDON

Россия должна сидеть в рядке и не высовываться.

Title: Alexander Gordon
Client: Alexander Gordon
Garrievich

1 | 3
2 | 4

1
Title: **Gallery Blanchaert**
Client: **Gallery Blanchaert Milan**
2
Title: **Obama**
Client: **Illustrative 2010 Berlin**
3
Title: **Moooi**
Client: **Moooi Gallry Amsterdam**
4
Title: **Grey Parys**
Client: **Grey Advertising Paris**

HENRY OBASI

Henry Obasi graduated from the visual communication and design department in the Central Saint Martins College of Art and Design. His commissioned works for Sony years ago were awarded and are still much talked about today. Nowadays, Henry Obasi has established himself in this industry, and started to become recognized by high-end clients as one of the most promising young illustrators. He has extended his influence in the music, fashion, design and advertising fields. Henry Obasi's illustrations are simple but thought-provoking, mirroring social reality. His works are intended to capture what really happens in the world by means of graphic diary.

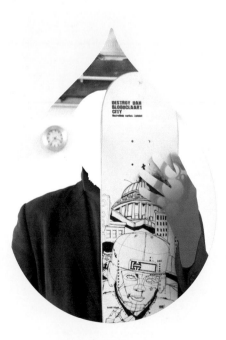

1 **When did you make up your mind to work as an illustrator? What happened then?**

I decided to start illustrating when I had had enough of stacking shelves in a supermarket and my back started to creak from the heavy lifting.

2 **Please summarize your design concept. What has contributed to your current style?**

There really isn't a design concept, just a vision to try and produce good work. Current style…. If I had to choose one "style" contributing to my work, it would be the "comic book genre."

3 **Where do you usually find the inspirations for your works? In other words, what do you usually do in the stage of design?**

Comics, paintings, photos, my children, music, crap TV, films, books, good TV, a chat with fellow designers over a drink, old magazines, music videos, vintage posters, computer games, etc, all form the initial stage for any project I am involved in.

It all starts with research.

4 **What do you think of the relationship between the artistic value and commercial value of the illustrations?**

They are both completely interchangeable.

5 **Have you found any conflict between drawing for your own fun and doing a commissioning work? How do you think the commercial operation has promoted this artistic creation?**

These days I rarely have time to draw for fun, so conflict is kept to minimum.

6 **Nowadays, how can an illustrator be successful both in the artistic sense and the commercial sense? Do you have any experience to share with us?**

First and foremost, an illustrator needs to make sure they can draw before worrying about their commercial/artistic value.

7 **As an illustrator, how do you interpret the role you are playing?**

To communicate the client's idea as clearly as possible.

8 **What's your icon in the artistic arena? What is the ultimate artist ideal to you?**

Icon….there are too many to name. "Ultimate Artist Ideal"…hmm…let's just say, "to do damn fine work."

9 **In what way do you think the illustration industry has changed? What do you think of the future trends in this industry?**

Illustration as a craft has become cheaper to produce, and unfortunately this trend will continue, forcing it to disappear as a realistic fulltime career.

Title: **Oasis**
Client: *Fly* Magazine

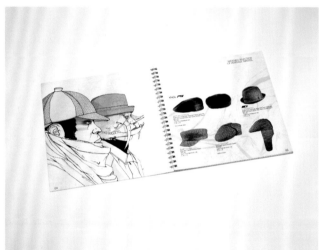

die wirtschaft

Nr. 6
Juni 2009
Euro 5,99

Das KMU⁺ Magazin: Service + Trends + Netzwerk   **Der Wirtschaftsverlag** | BUSINESS-TO-BUSINESS COMMUNICATIONS

9 007721 111009 06

Keine Panik!

Wie Führungskräfte jetzt die Nerven behalten

1   2

1
Title: **Music is….Poster** campaign
Client: **Fuse TV USA**

2
Title: **Panik**
Client: *Die Wirtschaft* Magazine

Die Exportchance lebt!
Wie KMU im Ausland punkten Seite 14

Gerry Keszler
Das Networking des Life-Ball-Machers Seite 44

P. b. b. Verlagspostamt 1050 Wien, Zul.-Nr. GZ 02Z030737 M   Postnummer 5   **www.wirtschaftsverlag.at   www.die-wirtschaft.at**

1
Title: **21 Dunk Salute**
Client: **Nike ID (rest)**
2
Title: **Student Travel**
Client: *Ryan Air* **Magazine**

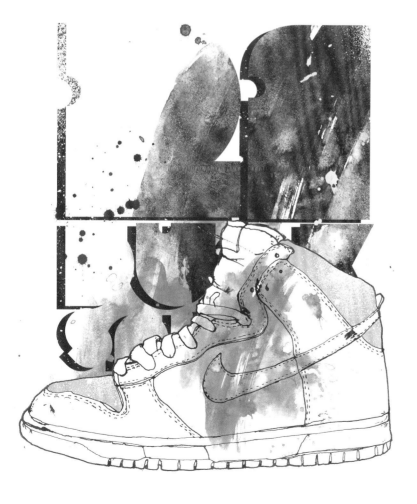

LOTIE

Born in Cole, France, Lotie is a professional illustrator who currently lives and works in Paris. Through years of practice, she has established a set of styles in her works, which are detailed as in traditional line drawing and gracefully pleasing. She firstly employs pencil, fountain pen and common inks in her illustration and incorporates her sketches and photos in later phases. She uses her favored gentle curves to create animals and plants, which fill the entire picture, vibrant, powerful but permeating with feminine sensitivity. In recnet years, her works have made active presence in publications and galleries throughout the world, making her a rising star in the illustration industry.

1 **When did you make up your mind to work as an illustrator? What happened then?**

I started my job in 2003. I didn't at all follow the studies appropriate to my job. I've got a degree in History and History of Art, and a Master's in Communication from the Sorbonne University in Paris. Then I did some training courses in companies. This was a "revelation" for me - it didn't suit me at all!

I was working with creative people and designers... And it was their job that I wanted to do! I decided to gather information on existing jobs in this field, and I went towards illustration!

I started then to put together a book in order to present my work to potential customers. I gave myself one or two years to see if it could work, if I had some success or not. By luck it worked quickly. I was soon contacted to participate in artistic projects as well as more and more traditional projects. My first orders made me believe in my capacities and encouraged me to pursue it.

2 **Please summarize your design concept. What has contributed to your current style?**

A hand-drawing with Indian ink, scanned, and then mixed with photographs, texture, colors, etc.

A lot of curved and rounded lines, and plants, organic elements. I think that my style has partly built upon the books and engravings I was shown as a child such as illustrated books by Gustave Doré, Martin Schongauer and Albrecht Dürer's engravings; also books with modern artists' works like Aubrey Beardsley and René Lalique's jewellery all have contributed to my style.

3 **Where do you usually find the inspirations for your works? In other words, what do you usually do in the stage of design?**

The inspirations for my work are diverse! It can be a sudden feeling, a scent, but also an exhibit I see or music I hear, anything that brings a melody or a color to my mind.

And above all, what inspires me most is the music I listen to while I'm drawing.

4 **What do you think of the relationship between the artistic value and commercial value of the illustrations?**

I think they can very well go together and stimulate each other. What's of commercial value is not necessarily without artistic value and interest.

5 **Have you found any conflict between drawing for your own fun and doing a commissioning work? How do you think the commercial operation has promoted this artistic creation?**

I've never felt such a conflict. I'm lucky enough to do commissioning work for which I'm hardly ever expected to deeply change my style. Of course, this kind of work doesn't necessarily look like my more personal or artistic works, but in the end they are all basically of my own style.

Besides, what happens is that very often, the brands that commission you to work for them, are interested in the artistic side of the illustrator in order to better display their product, and add an "arty" touch to it!

6 **Nowadays, how can an illustrator be successful both in the artistic sense and the commercial sense? Do you have any experience to share with us?**

A few years ago, in France at least, it was hardly compatible to be both an illustrator and successful as an artist in art galleries, exhibits, etc. You had to choose: be an illustrator or be an artist; but not both at the same time.

Today things are changing, the two worlds are more linked together, more illustrators show their works in exhibits. I think any talented illustrator can potentially be a successful and talented artist, as long as they have good ideas...and time to carry them out!

Besides, if an illustrator is active and present in the art world, it will give him extra "aura" in the business world! Clients usually like and would look for that artistic side of the illustrator.

Title: **Absolut Vodka Raspberry**
Client: **Absolut Vodka**

7 As an illustrator, how do you interpret the role you are playing?

An illustrator gives more visibility and enhances a product or a brand. Illustrators put into shape the client's ideas and desires; they make them become true and real.

8 What's your icon in the artistic arena? What is the ultimate artist ideal to you?

This is a difficult question. I admire multidisciplinary artists! As to my icon, I'd say Leonardo da Vinci!

9 In what way do you think the illustration industry has changed? What do you think of the future trends in this industry?

There's a strong tendency to being interdisciplinary, to embrace a wide range of media. Illustrators need to know and master more and more means of expression if they want people to hear and see them!! Animation, video, photography....the list goes on! Mostly they can't be happy with just drawing today. The most talented illustrators touch everything!!

1   *2*   *3*

1
Title: **Aquatic Feather**
Client: **Le Cube, Issy-les-Moulineaux, France**
2
Title: **Nebula**
Client: **Le Cube, Issy-les-Moulineaux, France**
3
Title: **Meduse**
Client: **Le Cube, Issy-les-Moulineaux, France**

1 | 3
| 2

1
Title: **Illustration for Bloom magazine**
Client: *Bloom* magazine #18, editions Li Edelkoort
2
Title: **Chanel N°5**
Client: *Flavor* magazine, France
3
Title: **Illustration for die Zeit magazine**
Client: *die Zeit* magazine, Germany

1
Title: **L'attente**
Client: **Magda Danysz Gallery, Paris**
2
Title: **Candies**
Client: *Le bonbon* magazine, France
3
Title: **Walldrawing**
Client: **Li Edelkoort**

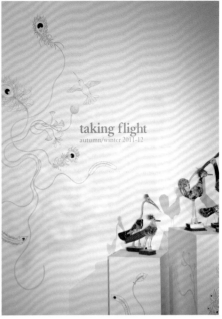

taking flight
autumn/winter 2011-12

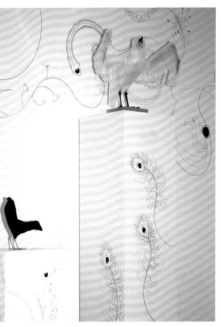

Avifauna (2010)
by Maarten Kolk & Guus Kusters
www.mkgk.nl

CATALINA ESTRADA

As a Latin American descent, Catalina Estrada has recently become one of the big names in the illustration industry. She has tactically integrated the vitality and passion that help to define the Latin America people with the grace and refinement featuring typical European style to create works that are highly striking in terms of color. According to Catalina, she herself is committed to capture emotional experience with dreamlike ambience, while employing complicated composition and dramatic aesthetics to highlight the dazzlingly brilliant Latin American civilization. Her evidently exotic style has attracted many fashion brands; even Paul Smith has been enchanted with the splendor in her works, and selected her illustrations as the motif, signifying her rewarding cooperation with commercial brands.

1 **When did you make up your mind to work as an illustrator? What happened then?**

I studied and worked for some time as a graphic designer. Without putting too much thought to it, clients started to call me and offer me jobs.

2 **Please summarize your design concept. What has contributed to your current style?**

As I said, I came from graphic design; thus, structure and colors are quite important in my work. I guess I am inspired by Latin American folk art, Asian folk art, arts and craft, etc...

3 **Where do you usually find the inspirations for your works? In other words, what do you usually do in the stage of design?**

I'm easily inspired by nature, by people, by everyday life, by many things, in fact, from literature, films and music. All this creates a bag of thoughts, so when a new project arrives I already have some ideas of what I want to do. Sometimes it is hard and sometimes it is quite easy.

4 **What do you think of the relationship between the artistic value and commercial value of the illustrations?**

I don't put too much thought to that. My feeling is that in many cases good illustration is well appreciated, so I guess that's an important thing.

5 **Have you found any conflict between drawing for your own fun and doing a commissioning work? How do you think the commercial operation has promoted this artistic creation?**

Well, on so many occasions I really enjoy my commissioned work, so it is not necessarily a question of fun. Sometimes I'd like to devote more time to my own stuff just to try new things, to have some freedom to play around.

As to the second question, I think they go hand in hand.

6 **Nowadays, how can an illustrator be successful both in the artistic sense and the commercial sense? Do you have any experience to share with us?**

I can't think of anything original....to be talented (whatever that may mean), work hard and take good care of the way you present your work.

7 **As an illustrator, how do you interpret the role you are playing?**

Well, it depends on the project, but in general, my satisfaction in the work is as important as the client's.

8 **What's your icon in the artistic arena? What is the ultimate artist ideal to you?**

Just working on your projects without worrying about anything else.

9 **In what way do you think the illustration industry has changed? What do you think of the future trends in this industry?**

The illustration industry will experience a great deal of prosperity in seven or eight years. The trends? ... I have no idea. But I hope this industry will attract more and more attention.

1-2
1 Title: **Paul Smith A / W 07 Collection**
2 Client: **Paul Smith**

1–4
Title: **Paul Smith A /
W 07 Collection**
Client: **Paul Smith**

1-7
Title: **Microsoft Zune Zodiac Series**
Client: **Microsoft**

1
Title: **CAMPER: Locus BCN**
Client: **Camper**
2-4
Title: **Paul Smith A/W 07 Collection**
Client: **Paul Smith**

1 | 3
2 | 4

1-4
Title: **Paulo Coelho Joy Diary**
Client: **Paulo Coelho**

EDUARDO
BERTONE

Since 1997, Eduardo Bertone,
the Argentine graphic designer,
illustrator and painter, has become popular in
Europe. He believes that illustration as an artistic
form can work as sedative in life and act as a way
of communication with the world. Eduardo Bertone's
works have been deeply influenced by pop art. This
artist has a consistent pursuit for experimentation and
has lived up to the manifesto of pop art — "let art be a
part of life, and daily life a part of art."

1 When did you make up your mind to work as an illustrator? What happened then?

I am always looking for new ways to express myself, trying different fields and media: I've worked as an art director for advertising and a graphic designer for more than 10 years. But over the last six years I've taken part in a lot of independent art projects where illustration was involved. And finally, a couple of years ago Anna Goodson Management (illustrator agent) contacted me to join them. I was so excited; it gave me courage to express myself mainly through illustration.

2 Please summarize your design concept. What has contributed to your current style?

I love fusion. I love merging all that I love with what catches my attention, taking the diversity and cultural richness we can find in all social and artistic expressions from around the world. I like to make people "travel" when they contemplate my art, not only to different places, but also ages, epoches: I use a childish drawing mixed with a traditional illustration, aboriginal art with fashion trend elements, sketches with labored illustration, a lot of different materials. It gives a dynamic atmosphere.

3 Where do you usually find the inspirations for your works? In other words, what do you usually do in the stage of design?

I find inspiration everywhere: maybe a stupid situation in the street; a child's scribble; graffiti on the door of a toilet; perhaps in a song, a movie or a book. If you're an artist it's important to be constantly aware of what's happening around you. And I am always doing something. In other words, "Inspiration exists, but it has to find us working," says Pablo Picasso.

4 Have you found any conflict between drawing for your own fun and doing a commissioning work? How do you think the commercial operation has promoted this artistic creation?

The art I create for commissioned projects should be as personal, implicated and committed as the art I make for myself. Commercial work has to also represent myself, it must have a part of me, and it's important to enjoy creating it. Otherwise it would be like any other job. On the other hand non-commissioned art has to be serious and committed. Everything I do is related to my life, my work and my passion.

5 Nowadays, how can an illustrator be successful both in the artistic sense and the commercial sense? Do you have any experience to share with us?

I've just launched a project with a Japanese partner, ROJI. The project is GUCHAGUCHA.COM. It's one example of what I do to succeed in avoiding companies; it's an independent project, commercial but directly related with art. You don't have to choose commercial or artistic, you can do both.

I think it's really important to keep doing art because it's what makes your commercial work unique. And it's also important to know how to get money from what you love doing, it's the only way to keep going. But I'm sure that money should never be the aim of your work.

Sometimes big companies make the mistake of forcing you to work a lot of hours a day; if you don't have time to create art or absorb what's happening around you, you will never do a great job. An advice, try to work for yourself.

6 As an illustrator, how do you interpret the role you are playing?

I never think about it, I just try to do what I love. And I think that's the point, if you love it, people will love it too.

Title: **101 Portraits for 101 Women**
Client: **Strawberry Frog NY Agency**

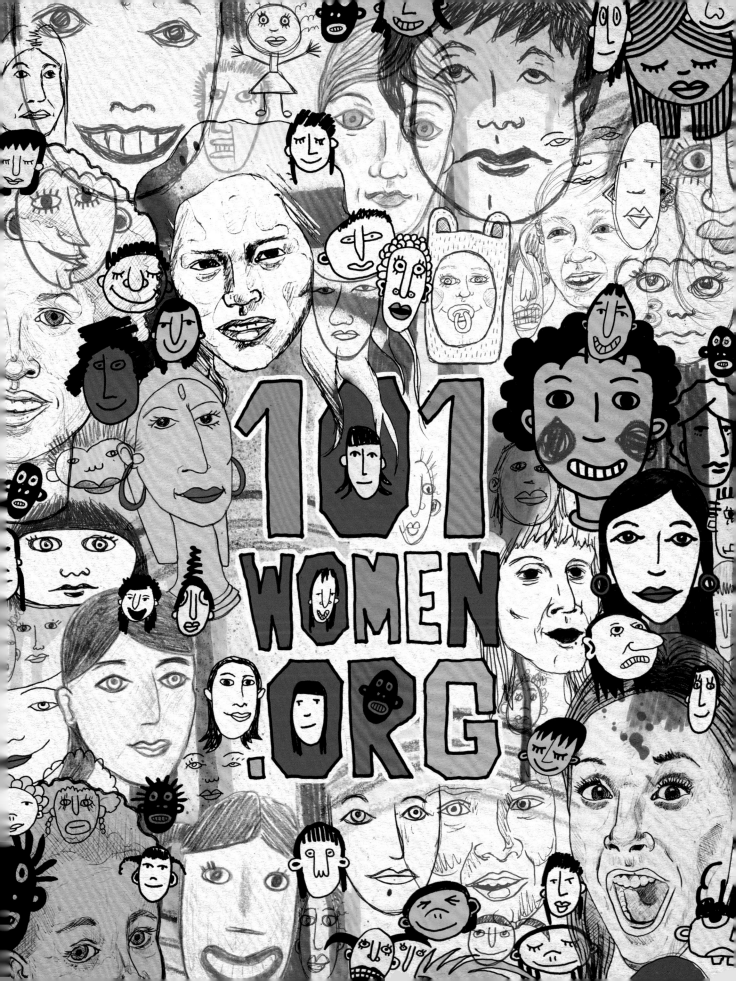

7 What's your icon in the artistic arena? What is the ultimate artist ideal to you?

Well, there are a lot of new artists doing really great work. But very few of them are in the contemporary art market scene. I belong to the "out art market" artistic movement. It's a movement where artists have to fight for themselves without a gallery or art managers' help. It's difficult to fight alone, but it's a way to have your own point of view. That's why this "movement" is getting more and more stronger lately, people are tired of "SAMO."

8 In what way do you think the illustration industry has changed? What do you think of the future trends in this industry?

The illustration industry has changed a lot. And I think in a good way. The Internet has a lot to do with it. Nowadays you can find uncountable illustrators on the net, and they are doing really good stuff; it's amazing. The evolution is disproportionate, with new trends and new ways coming everyday, every hour. Big companies have lost control, and now it belongs to people. Diversity is the new trend.

	2
1	3
	4

1
Title: **Let It Out**
Client: **Barnhart USA Agency**
2-4
Title: **Red and White labels**
Client: **Bear Flag Wines**

1
Title: Illustration for Belio 10th Aniversary Book
Client: *Belio* Magazine
2-5
Title: GUCHAGUCHA.COM
    (Project created with Japanese artist ROJI)
Client: GUCHAGUCHA.COM
6
Title: Promotional illustrations
Client: Anna Goodson Management

APFEL
ZET

Founded in Germany in 1996,
Apfel Zet Studio is made of Jarek
Spierpinski, Julia Bittner and Roman Bittner,
four energetic artists. Their works are inspired by
graphic design in the 1920s, and celebrate a modern and
paramount skills of expression, incorporating the traditional
and modern elements. Apfel Zet's works are compared to
"renovation mission" for the obvious antique style.

 When did you make up your mind to work as an illustrator? What happened then?

I never define myself as an illustrator and was not in the Illustrators class of Heinz Edelmann at the University of Fine Arts Stuttgart - but solved from the beginning all my graphical problems with illustrations. On the one hand, since I was a child the picture/illustration was always the main-medium to express myself; on the other hand, I like it that an illustration is much more personal than a photo or a pure typo-solution.

 Please summarize your design concept. What has contributed to your current style?

To be open for everything, and to love the world of graphic-design. I was inspired by all these famous graphic designers like Chris Ware, Cassandre, Winsor Mccay, Kamekura and Ludwig Hohlwein.

3 **Where do you usually find the inspirations for your works? In other words, what do you usually do in the stage of design?**

I find inspirations from the walls in the streets, television, cinema and books. Often I try to recollect things I dreamed of, create a "look" and see if it's fitting for the actual problem. In my mind I have a list of graphics I always wanted to do - and sometimes the possibility is there!

 What do you think of the relationship between the artistic value and commercial value of the illustrations?

I think I work like an artist in former times - before the age of modernism, before the cult of ingenuity. We have a client and he has a lot of ideas. We will negotiate, discuss and come to consensus.

5 **Have you found any conflict between drawing for your own fun and doing a commissioning work? How do you think the commercial operation has promoted this artistic creation?**

There is always a little conflict between doing commissioning work and drawing for myself because of the lack of time. Some clients want to boss you around. I don't like it but I have to support the studio and the family. Anyway, I will try my best to give full expression to my personal style.

6 **As an illustrator, how do you interpret the role you are playing?**

I am one of a new generation of designers and illustrators. We are a large team; we are children of the digital revolution; we use pictures from the internet; we are mixing everything up. We are very postmodern, very unheroic.

7 **What is your icon in the artistic arena? What is the ultimate artist ideal to you?**

A lot of people. One of them is Berlin Was Walton Ford. In a way he is an illustrator-artist, and never stops pushing the boundary. His styles range from large, vintage-looking, old school, to overwhelming and representational.
Another icon of mine is Karl Friedich Schinkel who was not only an architect but also a designer, painter and thinker. Generally speaking, I like artists whose work has a magic, megalomaniac and fantastic element like Winsor McCay, Raymond Hood, Elmer Dundy and Frederic Thompson, Walt Disney, the Beatles, Pete Townshend, Alfred Messel and Giles Gilbert Scott.

8 **In what way do you think the illustration industry has changed? What do you think of the future trends in this industry?**

In Germany illustration is just stepping out of the shadow of photography, which is quite good in my opinion.

Title: **Geld Spezial: Foresight**
Client: *DIE ZEIT*

5). *Dachs*

1 | 2

1-2
Title: GELD SPEZIAL - Dangers
Client: *DIE ZEIT*

1 | 2 3
  | 4 5

1
Title: **Like the Mafia**
Client: *Der Freitag*

2-5
Title: **Important Themes of the Future:**
 Energy, Communcation, Production, Mobility
Client: **Science Express Germany**

1-3
Title: **Geld Spezial: Foresight**
Client: *DIE ZEIT*

4). *Waschbär*

6). *Murmeltier*

b.) *Meeresschildkröte*

a.) *Schwebfliege*

3). Eichhörnchen

1
Title: **Plaza de Canalejas**
Client: **Madriz**
2
Title: **Overhead Trafficways**
Client: **Free work for the illustrative 07**
3
Title: **Now and Forever**
Client: **Free work for the illustrative 07**

POMME CHAN

Born in Bangkok, Thailand, the illustrator Pomme Chan was educated in London, and started to establish her own illustration style which features awakening of feminine awareness. Paper and painting pens are her constant companion at work; her passion about black ink is what inspires her; thriving plants, spiraling curves and interweaving vines are the key words to interpret her works. In 2002, Pomme Chan started to make success in Britain. According to the media, Pomme Chan "has a strong and special style. Pomme Chan is really an impressive and professional creator."

❶ When did you make up your mind to work as an illustrator? What happened then?

Since before I graduated from London College of Communication (LCC), London. All my work as a student involved illustration as the main medium, so I thought this is it. But the real turning point was when I moved to London 7 years ago, I saw things I've never seen in my country (Thailand) and I saw the potential of becoming an illustrator.

❷ Please summarize your design concept. What has contributed to your current style?

My style and concept tends to change from time to time. One thing people say about it is its feminine look, even though I sometimes try to change it. I guess that's when you have your style—I can't pin point what to call it—and that style/element always plays a big part in my work. Right now (2010) I'm obsessed with typography and fashion illustration; two years ago I was in love with drawing architecture and colorful stuff; before that it's all about doodle and swirl so I'm not sure what will be the next.

❸ Where do you usually find the inspirations for your works? In other words, what do you usually do in the stage of design?

Usually when I have a commercial brief in hand, I research for one day what I can draw that will best suit that project; otherwise, my sources could come from everyday life, nature, films, music and fashion.

❹ What do you think of the relationship between the artistic value and commercial value of the illustrations?

I think we need a balance there. I always like to put my thought and what I think is nice into commercial projects; but at the end, the brand and product has to sell. I like working on commercial as well as personal projects, though they are different ways of answering the brief but they are equally fun. I do think the Art-Director or whoever commissions the artist to do a commercial project should be aware of the artist's style so that they will get the best work from the artist without forcing them to change. I'm pretty lucky, most all of the people I work with understand that really well.

❺ Have you found any conflict between drawing for your own fun and doing a commissioning work? How do you think the commercial operation has promoted this artistic creation?

As I said above, sometimes conflict can happen when using the wrong people for the wrong project. But so far that's not happened to me yet. Commercial works promote artists in a different way, it's commercial, and they've got to sell. But I've seen so many great artists succeed in turning a great campaign into art. Also there is a change in the commercial world and audience, now they better understand the way illustration works and its value. They're more appreciative than they used to be.

❻ Nowadays, how can an illustrator be successful both in the artistic sense and the commercial sense? Do you have any experience to share with us?

Personally, I think we need to understand the background and purpose of both sides; compromise a little bit but at the same try to push the boundaries. Many times I did a personal piece then a client saw it on my site and they love it and they want something similar for their campaign. That's happened with many other artists too.

Title: **The Nature**
Client: **Microsoft Windows 7**

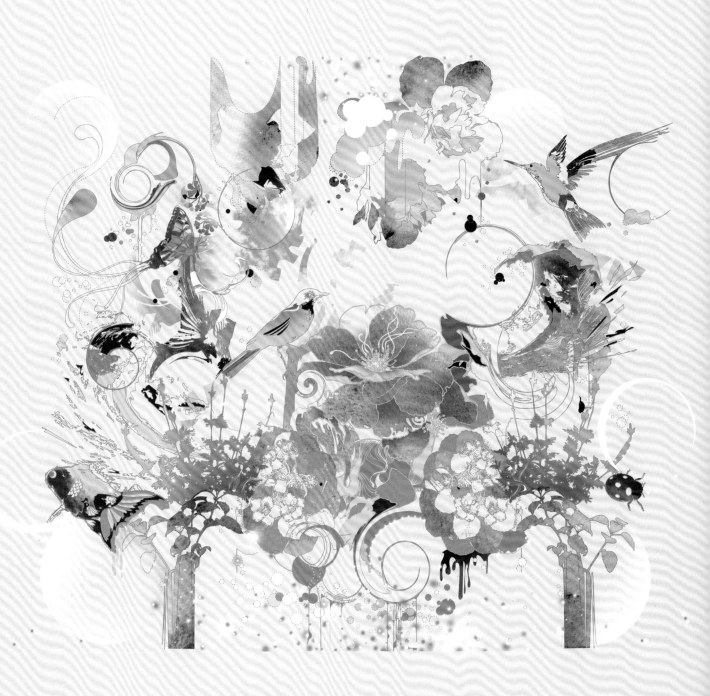

1-6
Title: **The Escape campaign**
Client: **Volkswagen**

7 As an illustrator, how do you interpret the role you are playing?

I'd say I'm just an image maker; I like using different medium — both computer and hand-drawn mix and match. I just hope that people enjoy my work. They don't need to understand it because most of the time I don't really have a deep concept, but I know what beauty is and I try to express the "beauty" in every piece I do.

8 What's your icon in the artistic arena? What is the ultimate artist ideal to you?

Oh, I adore many artists but no one in particular. Hmm....right now, Mario Hugo, Hello Von, Sean Freeman, Si Scott, non-format — they're all great works, personal and commercial.

9 In what way do you think the illustration industry has changed? What do you think of the future trends in this industry?

Now illustrations are everywhere. We used to see them only in magazines, ad campaigns, purely traditional drawing or very graphic, but now it's everything. It could be Illustration typographic, which makes typography more interesting. Illustration also plays a big part in the Fashion world too — you now see prints/patterns using illustration. There's nothing you can't apply illustration work to and I really mean it. Illustration developed in any technique such as 3D, computer generated, animation and mixed–media, and of course traditional hand-drawn is still here. I don't know the future trend and never really thought about it but I'm sure it will get more exciting.

1
2
3 4

1
Title: Topshop Illustreight
(wall painting and dress)
Client: Topshop
2-3
Title: Skiboard
Client: Atomic Skiboard by Tim Clayton
4
Title: Power of Plait (scarf)
Client: 111 days

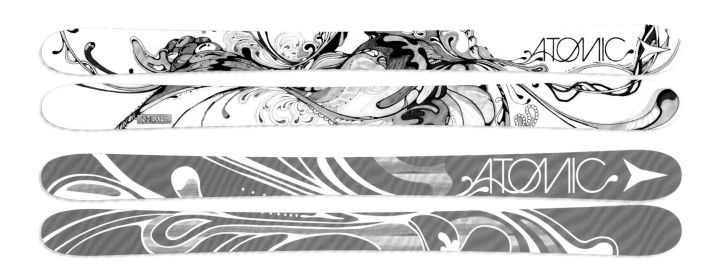

KAHORI MAKI

Kahori Maki from Japan prefers to convey oriental aesthetics permeating with Zen elements through plants, and has established her own "floral style." Featuring an obsession with the black color of various hues and different textures, her works are mostly black and white and are void of strong color. She has established her own creative process — she firstly does the tracing on water paper in an elaborate way by using ink and pencil, then cuts it down and has it scanned, and does the final composition on the computer, enabling repetitive use of each image to create a rich variety of ambience. Her clients include comme des garcons, Hoya Crystal, Levi's, Opeque, INAX, Shiseido, and NHK Orchestra.

1 When did you make up your mind to work as an illustrator? What happened then?
I was 5 years old. I just enjoyed drawing.

2 Please summarize your design concept. What has contributed to your current style?
I think I am drawing "life." I get so many inspirations from nature, and also human's energy.

3 Where do you usually find the inspirations for your works? In other words, what do you usually do in the stage of design?
When I wake up, I get lots of inspirations from somewhere.

4 What do you think of the relationship between the artistic value and commercial value of the illustrations?
It should be beautiful harmony.

5 Have you found any conflict between drawing for your own fun and doing a commissioning work? How do you think the commercial operation has promoted this artistic creation?
I just enjoy communication with whoever gives me a chance to work. It doesn't matter either for commercial purpose or private collection.

6 Nowadays, how can an illustrator be successful both in the artistic sense and the commercial sense? Do you have any experience to share with us?
You have to look through yourself closely.

7 As an illustrator, how do you interpret the role you are playing?
Visual communication.

Title: **2010 S/S ARMATINE**
Client: **SOMA Design**

1
2 | 3

1-2
Title: **Illustration for dining bar**
Client: **SABAKU no BARA**
3
Title: **Rakù Navi Art Car Collection 2007**
Client: **Pioneer**

CONTAINER PLUS

Container PLUS is a creative group engaged in design and other artistic activities, whose members are all females — Patricia Niven, Nicola Carter, and Luise Vormittag. These illustrators have extended from 2D illustration into space art, photography, animation and performance, and have evolved into a multi-dimensional artistic group. Their feminine perspective and complicated decorative lines are remarkably impressive. Employing joyful lines, these artists are always exploring every possiblity and means of expression beyond graphic design. Their active and professional business mode also helps to establish their names in the commerical arena.

 When did you make up your mind to work as an illustrator? What happened then?

Our first joint project was an exhibition at the Notting Hill Arts Club, which got us nominated as one of Creative Review's "Creative Futures 2003." And the year 2007 saw us getting increasingly interested in the third dimension: we started experimenting with set design and installations and then photographing the results. We also started incorporating performative elements in our exhibitions and began thinking of the possibility of creating a 360-degree experience with our artwork, rather than just an image on a page. So we decided to join forces with photographer Patricia Niven and an ever changing team of talented set designers. From then on things really started falling into place.

 Please summarize your design concept. What has contributed to your current style?

Generally we aim to create something that on first impression is beautiful and elegant, but a closer inspection reveals a lot of absurd details, such as fat squirrels in bikinis, a dog dressed up as a devil, a man wearing a chicken costume, etc.

Our current style has really gathered momentum since we joined forces with photographer Patricia Niven. And on many of our projects we have joined forces with a range of talented creatives that has pushed our skill set further.

 Where do you usually find the inspirations for your works? In other words, what do you usually do in the stage of design?

We usually start every project by having a long conversation mixing our ideas with the latest gossip, looking at all sorts of magazines ranging from *Art Monthly* to *Heat*. Somewhere in that conversation, in between our mediocre jokes, misunderstandings and a pile of magazines lies the seed of an idea.

 What do you think of the relationship between the artistic value and commercial value of the illustrations?

We will always explore the ideas we love. We devote time to personal and experimental projects, enabling us to explore techniques and develop new ideas, which then inform our commercial work.

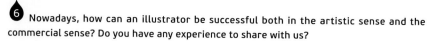 **Have you found any conflict between drawing for your own fun and doing a commissioning work? How do you think the commercial operation has promoted this artistic creation?**

Our experimental projects are always our unleashed, unrestrained vision where we don't have to worry about commercial viability or client feedback. We manage to sneak in elements of our experimental work but it would tend to be a more consumer-friendly version.

 Nowadays, how can an illustrator be successful both in the artistic sense and the commercial sense? Do you have any experience to share with us?

I think its about balance in your portfolio, you have to have enough commercial projects that can pay your bills and prove your value as a successful commercial artist, so that future clients have faith in your ability to carry out a project, but this has to be balanced with keeping your imagination and desire alive to create crazy sets and installations where its not about the money or the success.

7 As an illustrator, how do you interpret the role you are playing?

Illustration will always be a tool that enables us to create an experimental world where we can play with fantasy lands of large teacups, squirrels in bikinis and enchanted forests.

Title: **Go Global**
Client: **Beauty Mecca Cosmetica**

1

2

1
Title: **Go Global**
Client: **Beauty Mecca Cosmetica**

2
Title: **Oversized T-shirt design**
Client: **Wagamama restaurant chain**

1-2
Title: **Maxima - Jahreshoroskop**
Client: **Maxima's Jahreskhoroskop 2010**

KAROLIEN VANDERSTAPPEN

Karolien Vanderstappen is a lovely girl living in Brussels, Belgium. She loves drawing yellow ponies, tigers, bunnies, houses, cats and trees. She admits that what she depicts in her works has a lot to do with her own experience. Pencils, scissors and paper are the instruments for her clipping language; inspirations from outdated maganizes and rich imagination drive her creation. She uses a loony clipping style to compose a reverie of illustration. "Long live imagination!" is what she has lived by!

1 When did you make up your mind to work as an illustrator? And what happened then?

In fact I wanted to study fashion design, but I didn't like the atmosphere in those departments and felt a little bit lost. Finally, I started 3D design ceramics, inspired by a woman ceramist in my hometown. In that first year I was the only student — studying ceramics seems not to be really popular. I had a wonderful teacher who let me search out what I really wanted. In the same school I saw the works of the students of illustrative design and I liked it so much. The second year I changed to this direction; and yes, I loved it and I still do. So in a way, being an illustrator, it just happened. And it seems to be the right thing to do in my life. As a child I was always drawing and writing stories. Illustration is the sequel on my childhood. It makes me really happy. It's my way of expression.

2 Please summarize your design concept. What has contributed to your current style?

Do I have a concept? I'm rather an intuitive type. My concept is to follow my intuition when I'm drawing. The things on the paper, they're just happening. Expression guides your inner world out; that's my concept.

3 Where do you usually find the inspirations for your works? In other words, what do you usually do in the stage of design?

Inspirations? In fact it is my own feelings, my own experiences in life. When something goes wrong, bad love stories, for example, drawing helps me to feel happy again, to moderate things. But also stories of good writers are an inspiration, or sometimes some crazy things in the newspaper. Music helps me too. I'm always listening to music while I'm drawing. I'm searching for a certain emotion between my CDs; it helps me to go a level deeper in my illustrations. And encyclopedias of animals! They are always an inspiration to me. I like to draw animals, because they make the story more surrealistic.

4 What do you think of the relationship between the artistic value and commercial value of the illustrations?

Hmm, a difficult one. The best is when they come together, artistic value = commercial value. It happened a few times, that I made some free drawings and then people wanted to use them for a certain project, so the commercial thing came after. And that's nice! I worked one year as an illustrator for a culture center "De Spil" in Roeselare and they gave me so much freedom; then the artistic value is almost the same as the commercial value = BIG SMILE, lucky illustration feeling.

5 Have you found any conflict between drawing for your own fun and doing a commissioning work? How do you think the commercial operation has promoted this artistic creation?

Yes, it's a big conflict. My mind is not really commercial. People ask me for my specific style. If they ask for another style...then I have problems because I simply don't know how to do it. Then I'm really stressed and start to eat too much chocolate. I have a job as a teacher too, along with my job as an illustrator and probably I always will. I prefer commissioned works with an artistic value; I don't like to do illustrations only for money. Then I say "no." And I can say no, because I have another full-time job next to it to earn money to live my life. It's my dream to work part-time as an illustrator and part-time as a teacher. I believe the future will make this dream come true. I believe in believing :)

6 Nowadays, how can an illustrator be successful both in the artistic sense and the commercial sense? Do you have any experience to share with us?

Just do what you feel to do. Do what makes you happy. And be patient. Give yourself time to grow as an illustrator. One day your artistic illustrations can become commercial illustrations without losing their artistic value.

Title: **My dear deer**
Client: **De Banier, Belgium**

7 As an illustrator, how do you interpret the role you are playing?

As an illustrator I want to play a role of expression. Everybody needs his or her own way of expression. As a teacher in art, I play the role of the supporter of expression.

8 What's your icon in the artistic arena? What is the ultimate artist ideal to you?

When I was still studying I liked Sara Fanelli, and a few people have said I might be influenced by her. Yes, she's an icon; she was an important figure in my evolution to become an illustrator. But I also like artists such as Miranda July, Henry Darger and a lot of Dada-artists. I like people who do one thing on their own rhythm, who LOVE doing what they're doing. My shoemaker for example, he really loves to make shoes and that's so beautiful to see! So he's also an inspiration.

9 In what way do you think the illustration industry has changed? What do you think of the future trends in this industry?

I noticed that Belgium is not the "perfect" place to work as an illustrator. When I see the illustration-scene in the U.K. and France, oooh! I hope one day some publishers in Belgium will be ready to publish children's books with more artistic value. I have the opinion that some publishers here have become even more conservative in the last years. And if this does not change, I think I will have to move....Luckily, we have the Internet to travel and to follow the illustration-scene all over the world.

PAPA
OP ZOLDER

ZIJN TIJD ZOU NOG WEL KOMEN
OP EEN DAG ZOU HET ZOVER ZIJN

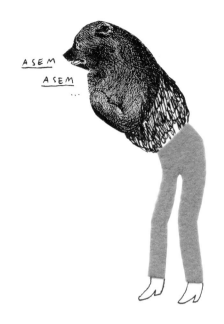

ASEM

ASEM

...

BEER WURMT ZICH IN EEN SLIM FIT JEANS.
EN DRAPEERT ZIJN VET VAKKUNDIG ALS HIJ IS
OVER DE BROEKSRAND.

BEER

KAN HEEL ERG GOED
NAAR BOVEN SPUWEN.

DENISE VAN LEEUWEN

Born in a painter's family, Denise Van Leeuwen lives and works in Rotterdam, Holland. In 2006, she worked for *Elle* and *Vogue* magazines as a freelance illustrator, and started to gain fame. She celebrates natural drawing style, and abhors any trace of computer processing. Inspired by beauty billboards in the 1960s, her works are mostly single-width portraits featuring a fashionable, brilliant and simple style. She is proficient at using a rich variety of expressions to highlight the character's personality.

1 When did you make up your mind to work as an illustrator? What happened then?

That's a short story. I've always wanted to draw and paint and color and glue. It's my calling. I couldn't stand it if another kid was better in drawing a tree. So I practised and practised until I got it right. I wanted to be a comic artist, or to work for Disney when I was older. I went to art school to become an illustrator and there, in my final year I met my current agent and she encouraged me to go freelancing. So I knocked on a few digital doors and got freelance jobs at *Elle* and *Avantgarde*. Whitin a year I could make a living as an illustrator.

2 Please summarize your design concept. What has contributed to your current style?

I feel very passionate about authenticity and I find that in drawing my illustrations by hand. Although I use Photoshop for small adjustments, the final artwork won't differ much from my original drawing. If an advertisement shows copied elements like, for instance, watersplashes in two places that are excactly the same (this really happened!) and it's meant to be covered up, I will see it. And it annoys me. I'd rather put some more time and effort in a piece then use the clonestamp to fake my style. I feel that if it looks handdrawn, it should be.

3 Where do you usually find the inspirations for your works? In other words, what do you usually do in the stage of design?

Lately I've been sketching a lot in my moleskine, before I get to the real thing. That's a new experience for me.

4 What do you think of the relationship between the artistic value and commercial value of the illustrations?

I try never to let the commercial value stand in the way of the artistic value. That doesn't always work out, sometimes I am merely executing what the client wants and that might fill your bank account, but it doesn't make me love what I do. I find that the most artistic illustrations come from the low-budget commissions. Therefore I'm not letting the money influence the effort I put in my work. I'm sure it pays back eventually.

5 Have you found any conflict between drawing for your own fun and doing a commissioning work? How do you think the commercial operation has promoted this artistic creation?

I love both worlds. I need commissions to keep it flowing. Not only for the pay; it makes me do things and meet people I otherwise wouldn't have and that can be very inspiring! Drawing for my own fun is about figuring out what I want to say and do.

6 Nowadays, how can an illustrator be successful both in the artistic sense and the commercial sense? Do you have any experience to share with us?

I think I'm very lucky that I can do what only feels natural to me, draw the way I love to, and be able to use that to make a living. I can't always find time to draw for fun, only when I'm on vacation I can.

7 What's your icon in the artistic arena? What is the ultimate artist ideal to you?

Vania Zouravliov. He doesn't even own a website, at least I couldn't find it. For me that shows how dedicated he is to his work. Take a look at the dozens of freakishly awesome artworks he has made. If only I could draw like that...

8 In what way do you think the illustration industry has changed? What do you think of the future trends in this industry?

The new kids are going to be so much more adapted to making computer arts, and the technology will be easier to use. I'm sure 3D renderings will become more and more a part of the industry. Not that it's my personal favourite, I'm still in love with the tangible pencil on paper.

1
Title: **No Golfer**
Client: *Fused* Magazine

2
Title: **Interview**
Client: *Rails* Magazine

1
Title: Night Train
Client: *Rails* Magazine
2
Title: Merry Christmas
Client: Personal work
3
Title: Jealousy
Client: Hodder & Stoughton
4
Title: Housekrant
Client: Housekrant
5
Title: xxx from Amsterdam
Client: Personal work

NALDEN.NET

YOSHI
TAJIMA

Yoshi Tajima is a graphic designer and illustrator from Tokyo. He loves cats, curry, and listening to the music in the midnight. When looking at his works, people might assume that the works were done by a female artist. However, what's amazing about Yoshi Tajima is that he is good at illustrating the feminine grace and elegance from a male perspective, highlighting their sexual appeal. Female characters in his works are always charming in a subtle way, presenting poetic visual enjoyment. He strives to capture fragile beauty and elusive moments. He has become a favorite of various fashion magazines due to the fashionable and emotional elements in his works.

1 When did you make up your mind to work as an illustrator? What happened then?

2004. I became an illustrator.

2 Please summarize your design concept. What has contributed to your current style?

Fantasy.

3 Where do you usually find the inspirations for your works? In other words, what do you usually do in the stage of design?

Reading books, watching movies, meeting people, and daily life.

4 What do you think of the relationship between the artistic value and commercial value of the illustrations?

For me, it is a matter of feeling. However, it is a matter of cash.

5 Have you found any conflict between drawing for your own fun and doing a commissioning work? How do you think the commercial operation has promoted this artistic creation?

Regulations sometimes make me sick, but it sometimes helps new creation.

6 Nowadays, how can an illustrator be successful both in the artistic sense and the commercial sense? Do you have any experience to share with us?

I am still struggling with this issue.

7 As an illustrator, how do you interpret the role you are playing?

Interpreting unconsciousness.

8 What's your icon in the artistic arena? What is the ultimate artist ideal to you?

Surrealist.

9 In what way do you think the illustration industry has changed? What do you think of the future trends in this industry?

It has become easy to catch up with someone else's style. Every man is the maker of his own fortune. I do not know about the future trend.

Title: **Figures**
(Partnered with Tomoko Tsuneda)

1-2
Title: **Dress**
Client: **Sony Computer Entertainment**

1
Title: **Chemical Sweet Girl**
Client: **Personal work**
2
Title: **Wild Style**
Client: **Personal work**

KUANTH

Kuanth has absolute loyalty for design arts. According to him, he is "a person who likes daydreaming…and enjoys being surrounded by beautiful and creative things." He is in the first place an experienced graphic designer, and had been engaged in this area for years. He used to work in a famous international advertising agency. The year 2002 witnessed the beginning of his illustration career. As a graphic designer and illustrator, he has learnt a lot through cooperation with a number of renowned brands in this brand-new area, including Nokia's L'AMOUR line, and Motorola's M1 line. His illustrations are highly practical, adaptable, and flexible, representing his infinite potential and immense imagination.

1 **When did you make up your mind to work as an illustrator? What happened then?**
I've always enjoyed doing different things: I started in the publishing industry, then moved on to advertising, followed by illustration and now I'm the owner of a cafe. I never really made up my mind to be an illustrator, it just happened along the way. Illustration is just one of my many interests — typography, photography, graphic design, product design, fashion, food, baking… the list goes on.

2 **Please summarize your design concept. What has contributed to your current style?**
Unfortunately when it comes to commercial jobs, I still don't have much say in terms of art direction or illustration style simply because clients are not ready to be adventurous with their projects. For personal work I tend to be obsessed with elements that are a bit more unusual with a sense of quirkiness and dark humor, as these two qualities capture more of my attention than others.

3 **Where do you usually find the inspirations for your works? In other words, what do you usually do in the stage of design?**
Inspiration comes from anywhere and everywhere, travel, books, movies, songs, food, human interaction, etc. In the stage of design, it's important for me to digest as much as possible — the intent of the project and what I want to achieve for the outcome. Normally the first idea that occurs will turn out to be my favorite so it's very spontaneous and subjective at the same time, as it may or may not please my clients. Also, others might not share the same point of view in which I strongly believe.

4 **What do you think of the relationship between the artistic value and commercial value of the illustrations?**
I think when it comes to commercial work, artistic value almost always takes the back seat and it is very hard (but important) to find a good balance between the two. After all, clients are the ones paying to get their job done and they are responsible for the brand and image they are representing.

5 **Have you found any conflict between drawing for your own fun and doing a commissioning work? How do you think the commercial operation has promoted this artistic creation?**
Always! There's always a conflict between personal and commercial work. I strive harder to make my personal work even more profound every time after I finished up a commercial project as a way to channel unexpressed creativity.

6 **Nowadays, how can an illustrator be successful both in the artistic sense and the commercial sense? Do you have any experience to share with us?**
If you can sell your artistic point of view with a marketing strategy, then you will be a very successful illustrator. Unfortunately, I'm still learning.

7 **As an illustrator, how do you interpret the role you are playing?**
I think it's always fun to see how you can inject your personality into a commercial job. That's also the most challenging part as an illustrator.

8 **What's your icon in the artistic arena? What is the ultimate artist ideal to you?**
Nagi Noda. She was such a genius as she could always wow us with her very personal touches in all the amazing work she left behind.

Title: **IDA Town**
Client: **IDA Singapore**
(Partnered with Sokkuan)

1 | 2

1
Title: **TongTong.sg**
Client: **Personal work**
2
Title: **Untitled**
Client: **Personal work**

FILIP PAGOWSKI

Born in Warsaw, Filip is the favorite illustrator of Rei Kawakubo. Featuring a unique perspective and brimming over with an untainted innocence, his works permeate with passion and simplicity. Filip solely depends on manual sketching to highlight primitve and unviolated beauty, acting as a defying force in an age when software technology dominates. He uses the simplest skills to maximize the power of his works. His unique artistic style has conquered the most stringent fashion world. Cooperating with Comme Des Garcons, Diane von Furstenberg and Li Ning has helped to build up his fame in his profession. In an age when flamboyance and impulsiveness prevail, Filip has interpreted "fashion" in a simple and naive way.

1 **When did you make up your mind to work as an illustrator? What happened then?**

At the end of 1980 I got to New York. I was very young, adventurous, a bit crazy and poor. I had four years of art school behind me but was still short of a diploma. I didn't care and wanted to start real life by getting work in graphics. Back in Poland I was studying poster design. I knew that in New York to do this or anything else close to the traditional idea of graphic design, wasn't at that moment realistic for me. On one hand I didn't have means to set up a proper studio with all it required in equipment, and on the other I didn't speak English good enough and didn't have legal papers to work fulltime for anybody else. Therefore I realized I could try working as a freelance illustrator. For that, all I needed was a bunch of pencils, some ink, a few brushes and some paper. Not much.

2 **Please summarize your design concept. What has contributed to your current style?**

I don't think I have a consciously defined design concept. I try not to think too much about it. Whatever happens happens naturally. All I focus on is honesty in my work. I work and think about work the way I feel and don't try to apply anybody else's idea to my projects.

Everybody has a certain set of sensibilities and if they use them correctly they should be able to naturally develop a style or a pattern of right impulses that might lead to a style. Life experiences, likes and dislikes among other things, mold our sensibilities.

3 **Where do you usually find the inspirations for your works? In other words, what do you usually do in the stage of design?**

Mostly, I get inspired by life. You see things and process them in your head, often not even knowing you are doing it. Then sometime later, depending on the occasion, something comes to your mind. Something that was there all along and seems appropriate at that very moment.

4 **What do you think of the relationship between the artistic value and commercial value of the illustrations?**

To make anything interesting it has to have an artistic element. Without it it's going to be boring. Regardless if it's a commercial job or an artistic one.

5 **Have you found any conflict between drawing for your own fun and doing a commissioning work? How do you think the commercial operation has promoted this artistic creation?**

No, I haven't. I don't change the way I draw when I change assignments. After all, the way I create is me. I'm not going to fake anything. I try to do jobs the best I can.

The commercial jobs have more promotional power, therefore they help a lot with all the other projects.

6 **Nowadays, how can an illustrator be successful both in the artistic sense and the commercial sense? Do you have any experience to share with us?**

One has to have talent, lots of luck and a willingness to be creative, try new things and never to feel fully satisfied.

7 **As an illustrator, how do you interpret the role you are playing?**

My role is to find the right answers to the multitude of visual challenges. Be it as a designer or illustrator.

1	2	**1/2/4**
3	4	Title: **Flower**
5	6	Client: **Comme des Garcons**

3/5
Title: **CdGmenTie**
Client: **CdG**

6
Title: **PlayBird**
Client: **CdG**

BLACK
BLACK
BLACK
BLACK
BLACK

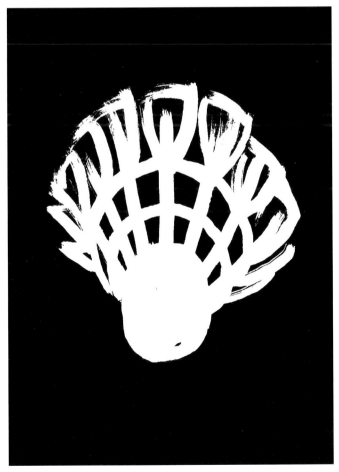

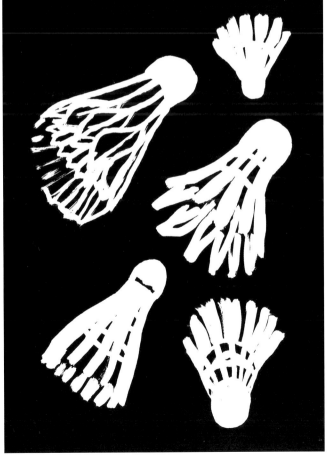

8 **What's your icon in the artistic arena? What is the ultimate artist ideal to you?**

There are quite a few artist that are close to my heart. I don't know if there is an ultimate artist, but if we talk about illustration/graphics and individualities, I have to mention Saul Steinberg.

Among the others I like are Catalan/Spanish painter, Antonio Tapies, I get inspired by his work; or Peter Breughel the Elder, who's paintings are like movies to me.

9 **In what way do you think the illustration industry has changed? What do you think of the future trends in this industry?**

Honestly, I think that the illustration industry sucks.... And I don't really care about its future trends. I try to stay away from the trends as I find them limiting and passing. But I hope the industry is going to expand to include broader, a more original and adventurous visual vocabulary.

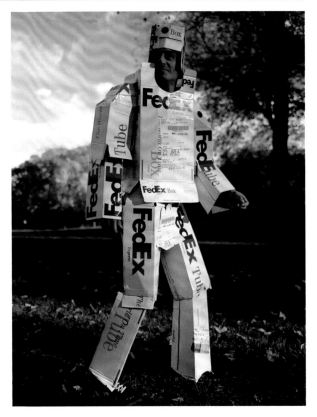

1	2		4	5
	3			6

1-3
Title: **Exhibition of Li-Ning**
Client: **Li-Ning**
4-5
Title: **Fly Time**
6
Title: **Filip PAGOWSKI**

JESSE AUERSALO

Jesse Auersalo is a Finnish illustrator and visual artist who currently lives in New York. He is obsessed with facial expressions, body language and old photos. His works are always cold, eerie, and surreal. He admits loving creating invisible and interesting things, and attempting to represent the classical and the contemporary in the same time and space. He loves depicting life and death. The black-and-white pictures feature refined lines, but the subjects are serious and depressive. The pictures and the subjects pose strong contrast with each other, leaving his works exuding a dramatic sense of absurdity. His drawing skills are so refined that his works look computer-made. However, he has kept it a secret.

1 When did you make up your mind to work as an illustrator? What happened then?

I had been working with graphic design for some time and I just realized that I was more happy doing illustrations. For me, giving up graphic design was easy. I had come to a point that I wasn't enjoying it as much as I did before.

2 Please summarize your design concept. What has contributed to your current style?

I came across these elements, surfaces and structures. It felt pretty natural and I gave it a try. Haven't got bored since.

3 Where do you usually find the inspirations for your works? In other words, what do you usually do in the stage of design?

In some case it might be carefully planned vision but sometimes I just get interested in random detail and start studying it.

4 What do you think of the relationship between the artistic value and commercial value of the illustrations?

Money.

5 Have you found any conflict between drawing for your own fun and doing a commissioning work? How do you think the commercial operation has promoted this artistic creation?

Once in a while they get together well. It just needs a certain type of commitment for the whole team that is working with the case. That everyone understands the values of each side — the creative and commercial side of it — all the way through the process. It's also pretty much about understanding a good balance of compromises.

6 Nowadays, how can an illustrator be successful both in the artistic sense and the commercial sense? Do you have any experience to share with us?

There are ways to get out there…. But still, at the end of the day it's pretty much the work itself that has to speak for itself.

7 As an illustrator, how do you interpret the role you are playing?

I don't take it too seriously…. I'm not into politics.

8 What's your icon in the artistic arena? What is the ultimate artist ideal to you?

Basically just being able to work on projects that doesn't limit my creative output, but instead opens possibilities for new opportunities. I'm always into something new.

9 In what way do you think the illustration industry has changed? What do you think of the future trends in this industry?

Now it's undoubtedly getting more into social communities, sharing things in platforms and collaboration.

Title: **Purple Wolf**
Client: *Untitled* **Magazine**

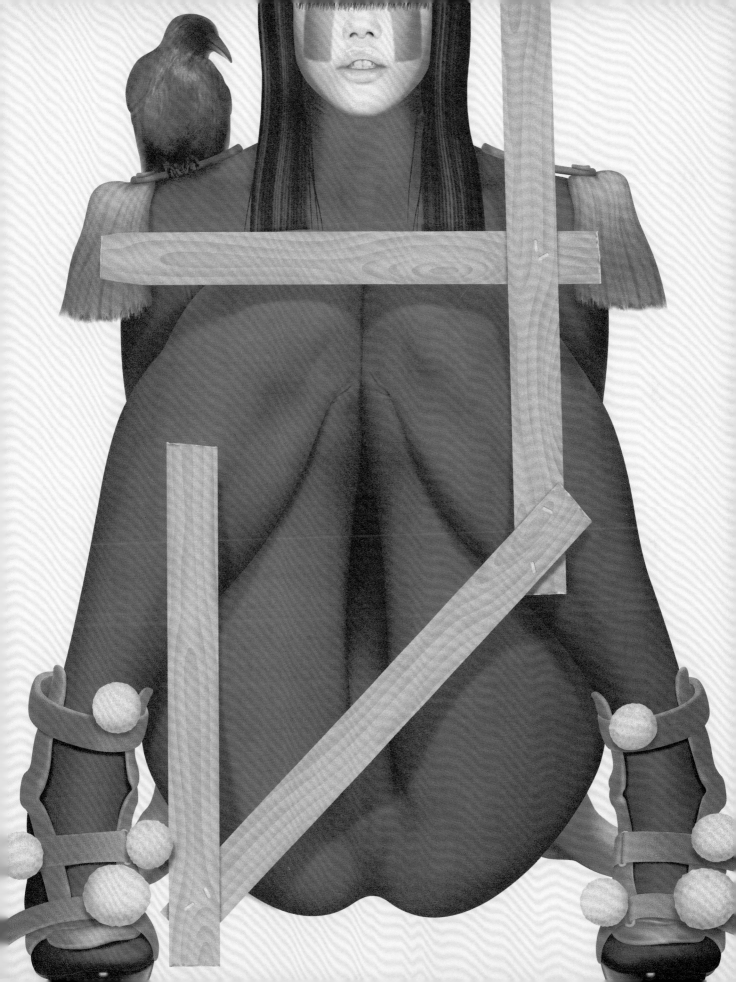

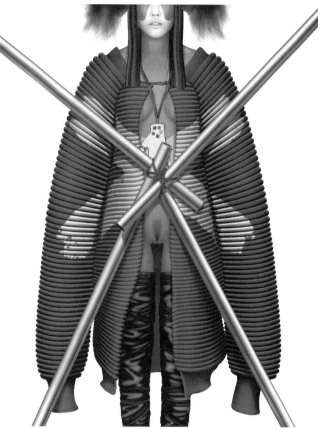

1-5
Title: **Purple Wolf**
Client: *Untitled* Magazine
6
Title: **Untitled**

Q&A Fax

We have invited twenty-six illustrators to make interactions through "graphic fax." Come and see how inspiring their answers are!

TO: 008601059521111   P: 1/6

08-AUG-2009 00:26   FROM: MARCOS CHIN

WELCOME TO THE NEW WORLD OF IDEAS

Q&A

To: CYPI
Attention: in&out
R.E.: QUESTIONS&ANSWERS
Date: 08/08/09

YOU'RE AN ODD LOOKING CREATURE

Who you are?
You can draw something here!

01: What does illustration mean to you? How do you define this term?

THE ART + BUSINESS of COMMUNICATION

02: Have you ever thought of putting your works into commercial use?

YES! YOU CAN DO IT!

DRAWING

CHOCOLATE

03: What is your favorite? Please give me six names.

pizza french fries flowers
ICE CREAM SANDWICHES
SNEAKERS mikee rita
moustaches DINOSAURS
vampires
DOCUMENTARIES
FASHION writing READING

SCARY MOVIES Boo Boo Boo

RELIGIOUS FUNDAMENTALISTS

04: What do you resent most? Please give me six names.

CREEPS! FALSE HUMILITY
INSENSITIVE PEOPLE
the U.S. healthcare system
LOUD TALKERS
NARROW MINDEDNESS
BIGOTS

05: Which artists do you like most?

NICK CAVE : YAYOI KUSAMA
WILLIAM KENTRIDGE
NEO RAUCH   be inquisitive
be curious

06: What do you think of yourself?

DON'T GIVE UP

DRIP DRIP DRIP

07: Can you tell us about what you always dream of doing?

08: Could you say something to our readers?

HELLO! FROM BROOKLYN

CALL YOUR MOM   IT'S FOR YOU

清水裕子
Yuko Shimizu
New York, NY, USA

Who you are?
You can draw something here!

Q&A

To: CYPI
Attention: in&out
R.E.:   QUESTIONS&ANSWERS
Date: 08/08/09

01: What does illustration mean to you? How do you define this term?

Life.

02: Have you ever thought of putting your works into commercial use?

well, that's all I do as an 'illustrator'...

03: What is your favorite? Please give me six names.

drawing , travel around the world , friends & family,
great design, New York City, 'Bruiser' the dog

let me
lick your
feet!

04: What do you resent most? Please give me six names.

?????

05: Which artists do you like most?

Just Waaaaaay too many to list!

06: What do you think of yourself?

I wish I knew.

07: Can you tell us about what you always dream of doing?

Become a Superhero and save the world (... Really???)

08: Could you say something to our readers?

Hello.

Q&A

To: CYPI
Attention: in&out
R.E.: QUESTIONS&ANSWERS
Date: 08/08/09

10

Who you are?
You can draw something here!

01: What does illustration mean to you? How do you define this term?

illustration isn't design, a lot of people make fuzz with these terms
Illustration is a way to make people pay attention in a text or a visual concept
people stop to see an interesting illustration.

02: Have you ever thought of putting your works into commercial use?

Yeah! of course. We need to pay our bills!

03: What is your favorite? Please give me six names.

1.) AHN... COURSE...   ☺

2.) ... OW..N..   ☻

3.) SSSSS... FAVORITTTE ...

4.) YEAH.. NAMES...

5.) UMHM... GUARANÁ

6.) WHATEVER.. I MAY ROAM (METALLICA) ◉◉

04: What do you resent most? Please give me six names.

1) CALL US BASE 5, ĩs V (VĩsuaL)

2) BUROCRACY

3) PEOPLE WHO DON'T PAY

4) WHEN THE PAPER IN THE PRINTER ENDS

5) ♦♦♦♦♦

6)

05: Which artists do you like most?

BEN GAZARRA, WALDICK SORIANO, DEISE TIGRONA AND ANNA KARINA. (WONDERFUL!)
BLU, BANKSY, FRANK ZAPPA, FELA KUTI, RODCHENKO, FRANCIS BACON, MILES DAVIS, JAN SVANKMAJER,
HERMETO PASCOAL

06: What do you think of yourself?

07: Can you tell us about what you always dream of doing?

08: Could you say something to our readers?

WØRK FOЯ FOOD, girls AND PARTIES

Q&A

To: CYPI
Attention: in&out
R.E.: QUESTIONS&ANSWERS
Date: 08/08/09

Who you are?
You can draw something here!

01: What does illustration mean to you? How do you define this term?

02: Have you ever thought of putting your works into commercial use?

03: What is your favorite? Please give me six names.

04: What do you resent most? Please give me six names.

05: Which artists do you like most?

Yoshitomo Nara.

06: What do you think of yourself?

07: Can you tell us about what you always dream of doing?

Traveling the world

08: Could you say something to our readers?

BE HAPPY !!

Q&A

To: CYPI
Attention: In&out
R.E.: QUESTIONS&ANSWERS
Date: 08/08/09

01: What does illustration mean to you? How do you define this term?

TRANSFORMATION?

02: Have you ever thought of putting your works into commercial use?

IN ☺)

ZOMBIE LOVE

03: What is your favorite? Please give me six names.

LOVE →

WORSHIP COLOUR?

KAMIKAZE

04: What do you resent most? Please give me six names.

iGNORANCE

05: Which artists do you like most?

ROBERT WILLIAMS + HIRONIMUS BOSCH + CARAVAGGIO + H.R. GIGER

06: What do you think of yourself?

THANX LIFE

07: Can you tell us about what you always dream of doing?

BUILDING A VANDAL ROBO (PAINT) WHICH I WILL CONTROL.

08: Could you say something to our readers?

BELIEVE IN YOURSELF !!!

Q&A

To: CYPI
Attention: in&out
R.E.: QUESTIONS&ANSWERS
Date: 08/08/09

Who you are?
You can draw something here!

01: What does illustration mean to you? How do you define this term?

DRAWING AT PUBLICS.
MY DOOR TO THE WORLD.

02: Have you ever thought of putting your works into commercial use?

IT'S MY BEST JOB!

03: What is your favorite? Please give me six names.

SUN WARMER JACKET AND LOVES

04: What do you resent most? Please give me six names.

IN: HOUSE HUSBAND
OUT: RESPECTFUL TEACHER AND ARTIST

05: Which artists do you like most?

SNOOPY(USA)

06: What do you think of yourself?

NICE GUY
NICE PEN

07: Can you tell us about what you always dream of doing?

TO GET A CAR
TO GET A BIG HOUSE AND GARDEN

08: Could you say something to our readers?

WHICH DO PREFER DESIGN OR ART
TEA OR COFFEE? RICE OR BREAD?

Q&A

To: CYPI
Attention: in&out
R.E.: QUESTIONS&ANSWERS
Date: 08/08/09

Who you are? I am Jon
You can draw something here! ok!

01: What does illustration mean to you? How do you define this term?

Art + Design + sometimes other things = ILLUSTRATION

02: Have you ever thought of putting your works into commercial use?

Yes I have. Other people have had that thought for me too.

03: What is your favorite? Please give me six names.

1. Tree   2. Conker   3. Bagel   4. Teapot   5. Spaceship   6. Snail

04: What do you resent most? Please give me six names.

1. Humans   2. Litter   3. Bad eggs   4. Maths teachers   5. My friend Niki   6. cold tea / mouldy cakes

05: Which artists do you like most?

ALL THE GOOD ONES

06: What do you think of yourself?

sunny but sad   young   COLD

07: Can you tell us about what you always dream of doing?

hi Jon, I love your doodles

kissing attractive movie stars

08: Could you say something to our readers?

Let's be friends!

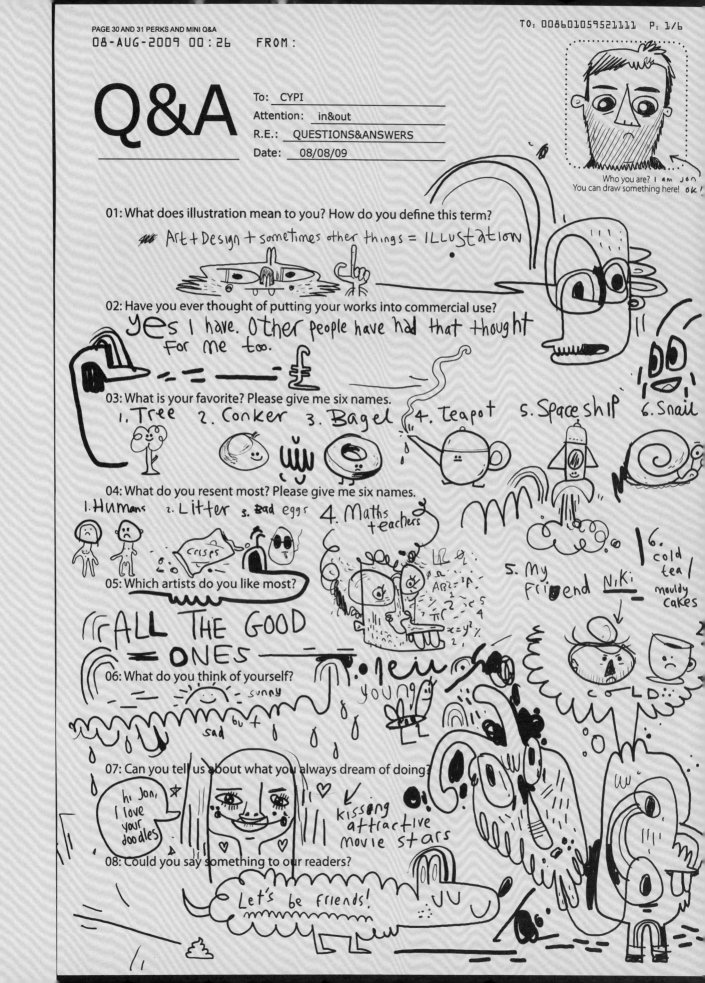

Q&A

To: CYPI
Attention: in&out
R.E.: QUESTIONS&ANSWERS
Date: 08/08/09

Who you are?
You can draw something here!

NICHOLAS DI GENOVA

01: What does illustration mean to you? How do you define this term?

- IT ALLOWS ME TO DRAW ALL DAY, WHICH IS MY FAVOURITE THING TO DO WITH MY TIME, SO IT'S PRETTY MUCH THE BEST. FOR ME, ILLUSTRATION IS ~~A~~ I DON'T KNOW HOW TO DEFINE ILLUSTRATION. I JUST DRAW EVERYDAY, SOMETIMES PEOPLE BUY ONE OF MY DRAWINGS, AND I GET ENOUGH MONEY TO LIVE OFF OF A LITTLE LONGER, SO I GET TO KEEP DRAWING THINGS- I REALIZE THAT SOUNDED STUPID, BUT THAT IS HOW I THINK OF WHAT I DO.

02: Have you ever thought of putting your works into commercial use?

I WANT TO DO CHARACTER DESIGN FOR ~~XXXX~~ MONSTER MOVIES AND NATURE DOCUMENTARIES.

03: What is your favorite? Please give me six names.

STRIPED,

HYENAS   WILD DOGS
BATS   HERMIT CRABS
CORMORANTS BUTTERFLIES

04: What do you resent most? Please give me six names.

OMELETTES (OR ANYTHING WITH LOTS OF EGGS)
COOKIES
CAKE

PANCAKES
CHOCOLATE
SOGGY LETTUCE

05: Which artists do you like most?

- LUKE PAINTER, MAT BROWN, ZAK SMITH, SHAWN CHENG, ANDREW WILSON, JAMIYLA LOWE, TRISTRAM LANSDOWNE, KRIS KUKSI, STEPHEN APPLEBY-BARR, ~~NICHOLAS~~ AOKI, ANDREW REMINGTON BAILEY, AMANDA NEDHAM, WINNIE TRJONG, PATRICK KRZYZNOWSKI, AND CHRISTY LANGER.

06: What do you think of yourself?

- I THINK I'M OK. ~~XXXXX~~

07: Can you tell us about what you always dream of doing?

- I GUESS I'M ALREADY DOING IT. ~~XXXXXXXX~~ I DRAW MONSTERS ALL DAY. I NAP WHENEVER I FEEL LIKE IT, I SHARE A STUDIO WITH MY BEST FRIEND. I LIVE ABOVE MY STUDIO WITH MY GIRLFRIEND. THIS IS WHAT I WANTED WHEN I WAS A KID, I'M REALLY LUCKY.

08: Could you say something to our readers?

I'M SORRY I MESSED UP THE HERMIT CRAB DRAWING.

Q&A

To: CYPI
Attention: in&out
R.E.: QUESTIONS&ANSWERS
Date: 08/08/09

I... I'm blanqu

Who you are?

01: What does illustration mean to you? How do you define this term?

food of my...eyes

02: Have you ever thought of putting your works into commercial use?

yes, I like Mechanical Reproduction

03: What is your favorite? Please give me six names.

toys-candy-Painting-drawing Body~Photography~~~

04: What do you resent most? Please give me six names.

Body Painting

05: Which artists do you like most?

J. BOSCH

06: What do you think of yourself?

i'm a good dogboy

07: Can you tell us about what you always dream of doing?

make a movie of my last dream

08: Could you say something to our readers?

Love your teeths

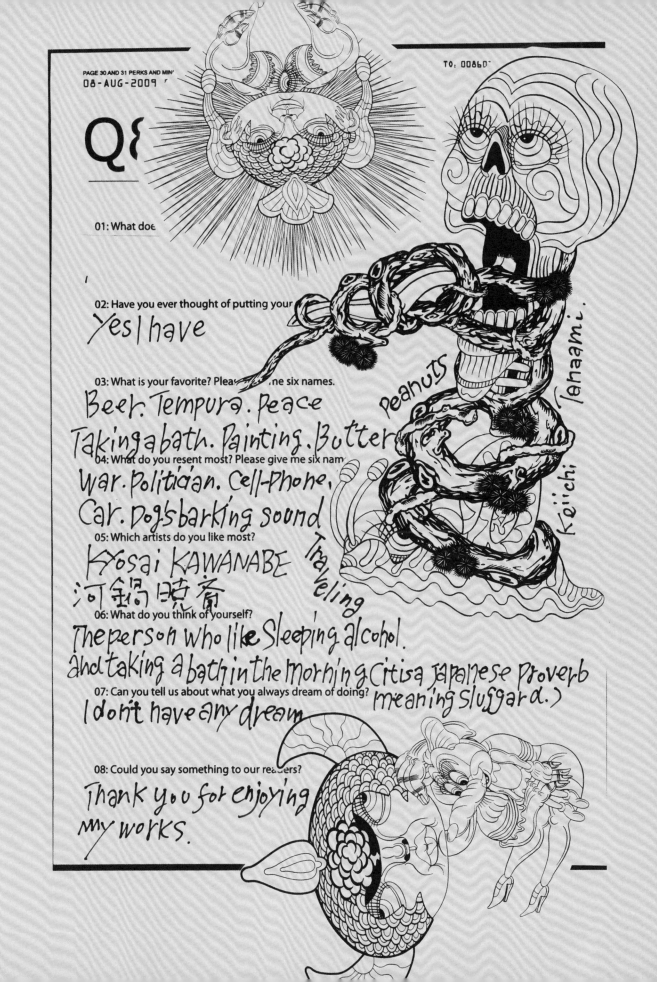

Q8

01: What doe

02: Have you ever thought of putting your

Yes I have

03: What is your favorite? Plea... ...ne six names.

Beer. Tempura. Peace
Taking a bath. Painting. Butter... peanuts

04: What do you resent most? Please give me six nam...

War. Politician. Cell-phone.
Car. Dogs barking sound

05: Which artists do you like most?

Kyosai KAWANABE
河鍋暁斎   Traveling

06: What do you think of yourself?

The person who like Sleeping alcohol.
And taking a bath in the morning (it is a Japanese Proverb
meaning sluggard.)

07: Can you tell us about what you always dream of doing?

I don't have any dream

08: Could you say something to our readers?

Thank you for enjoying
My works.

Keiichi Tanaami.

Q&A

To: CYPI
Attention: in&out
R.E.: QUESTIONS&ANSWERS
Date: 08/08/09

Hi I am eeshaun.

Who you are?
You can draw something here!

This is no an accura drawin of me.

01: What does illustration mean to you? How do you define this term?

Illustration is image-making - it is about creating a visual representation or drawing of something.

02: Have you ever thought of putting your works into commercial use?

Yes! On bags, clothes, toys.

03: What is your favorite? Please give me six names.

↘ what? ~~____~~ Musicians }
George Michael
D'angeLo
SADE
Earth Wind & FiRE
PRINCE
marvin gaye

04: What do you resent most? Please give me six names.

1.) The army   4.) The army
2.) The army   5.) The army
3.) The army   6.) The army

05: Which artists do you like most?

Maya Hayuk, David shrigley, Chris Johanson
Richard Colman, Jon Burgerman, Tim Biskup,

06: What do you think of yourself?

GREAT !

07: Can you tell us about what you always dream of doing?

Doing this - drawing & inspiring people.

08: Could you say something to our readers?

Thank you for buying & reading this - (I hope you didn't waste your time ....) Enjoy Life ! ♥

Q&A

To: CYPI

Attention: in&out

R.E.: QUESTIONS&ANSWERS

Date: 08/08/09

Who you are?
You can draw something here!

01: What does illustration mean to you? How do you define this term?
For me drawing and art that communicates.

02: Have you ever thought of putting your works into commercial use?
Most of the illustrations that are realizable for commercial use. Are published in magazines.

03: What is your favorite? Please give me six names.
Perrier , 59 demi brigade de ligne de marenco (Napoleonic army),
Renata Tebaldi, Caravaggio, Genoa Cricket and Football Club, San Rocco (Italy Genova)

04: What do you resent most? Please give me six names.
Sorry but my modest English, I understand the question.

05: Which artists do you like most?
Diego Rivera

06: What do you think of yourself?
 I try to survive.

07: Can you tell us about what you always dream of doing?
Dream concierge.

08: Could you say something to our readers?
It 's a great honor to present my work.

08-AUG-2009 00:26 • FROM:

TO: 008601059521111   P: 1/6

OBAKI Q&A

To: CYPI

Attention: in&out

R.E.: QUESTIONS&ANSWERS

Date: 08/08/09

Who you are?
You can draw something here!

01: What does illustration mean to you? How do you define this term?

BEST WAY → 2 MAKE A LIVING

02: Have you ever thought of putting your works into commercial use?

YES

03: What is your favorite? Please give me six names.

IF YOU MEAN ARTIST
DAVID MAZZUCHELLI, BASLEY
ALEX MALEV, SCHIELE
EVAN UGLOW JENNY SAVILLE

04: What do you resent most? Please give me six names.

I RESENT NOTHING !!!
[I RESENT NOTHING !!!]

05: Which artists do you like most?

LOOK AT QUESTION 3 QUESTION 03

06: What do you think of yourself?

I DONT "THINK"
I KNOW

07: Can you tell us about what you always dream of?

I AM DOING IT

08: Could you say something to our readers?

LIVE

Q&A

To: CYPI

Attention: in&out

R.E.: QUESTIONS&ANSWERS

Date: 08/08/09

Who you are?
You can draw something here!

01: What does illustration mean to you? How do you define this term?

It's an image that completes and helps describe an idea, a text, a topic... It can be fixed or animated. It can be very diverse in order to adapt to all kinds of media : a photograph, a drawing, a mix of both etc...

02: Have you ever thought of putting your works into commercial use?

Yes, I almost always do! I mainly work for advertising agencies and their clients who come from all kinds of different horizons. Most of my work is done in that perspective.

03: What is your favorite? Please give me six names.

eating / friends / holidays / traveling / be in love / Nature

04: What do you resent most? Please give me six names.

Intolerance / wickedness , lack of humor / boredom sadness / lack of respect

05: Which artists do you like most?

Gustave Doré, Martin Schongauer, Albrecht Dürer ... the work of the Modern Style artists (Mucha, Beardsley, Guimard...), Bernini's marble statues... but also new artists! It's difficult to name 1 or 2 artists. I like several artists in varied fields from the Antiquity to nowadays!

06: What do you think of yourself?

A hard-worker, a perfectionist, sometimes a tendency to pessimism and anxiety, but I also love laughing... and making people laugh!

07: Can you tell us about what you always dream of doing?

I'd like to make a global large-scale project! Sound, video/animation, static image, the whole mixed. I'd like to reach always more intricacies between the media. It would be something like a gigantic sound and light. The place would be as well a place of nature, a forest for instance, or a big city!

08: Could you say something to our readers?

More generosity, more creativity, more fantasy always!

08-AUG-2009 00:26   FROM:

TO: 008601859521111   P. 1/6

Q&A

To: CYPI
Attention: in&out
R.E.: QUESTIONS&ANSWERS
Date: 08/08/09

I'M CATALINA ESTRADA URIBE

Who you are?
You can draw something here!

01: What does illustration mean to you? How do you define this term?

- A VERY NICE WAY TO MAKE MY LIVING
- PUT LIGH INTO WORDS OR IDEAS.

02: Have you ever thought of putting your works into commercial use?

TOO LATE. IT'S ALREADY DONE. A LOT.
too lateeeeee....
MANY TIMES.

03: What is your favorite? Please give me six names.

- PANCHO   - TRAVELS
- FAMILY   - GOOD BOOK   I ♡ ALL THIS
- NICE FOOD   - SLEEPING

04: What do you resent most? Please give me six names.

- BAD COFFE   - WAR
- BAD PEOPLE   - WAKE UP EARLY   I HATE THIS
- INJUSTICE   - WHEN MY PLACE IS NOT TIDY

05: Which artists do you like most?

- PANCHO → MY HUSBAND   - ANNE BRUN
- NICO MY BROTHER   - M.WARD
- MY MOTHER   - VETIVER

06: What do you think of yourself?

I'M A NICE PERSON AND SOMETIMES I GET A BIT COMPLICATED.

07: Can you tell us about what you always dream of doing?

BEING ABLE TO SLEEP, TRAVEL AND HAVE LOTS OF FUN
ya LOT, ya LOT

08: Could you say something to our readers?

HELLOOOoooo READERS

HOLA, SHALOM, ALOHA, CONICHIWA, CIAO, SALAM ALEKUM,

SAVADIKA, NIHAO, CUCU, HEI BOK, NAZDAR, MERHABA, HAI, HEJ!!!!

To: CYPI
Attention: in&out
R.E.: QUESTIONS&ANSWERS
Date: 08/08/09

01: What does illustration mean to you? How do you define this term?

TO KEEP IN TOUCH WITH OUR INNER CHILD

02: Have you ever thought of putting your works into commercial use?

AH .... YES!

03: What is your favorite? Please give me six names.

OUR TWINS MIA & NEMO, HAVING A COFFEE AFTER BRINGING THEM TO KINDERGARDEN, COOKING & EATING, GUITAR SOLOS, HIGH HEELS, SUMMER

04: What do you resent most? Please give me six names.

ELECTRONIC MUSIC, DARK CHOCOLATE, TRAINEES, WHO DON'T LIKE TO DRINK COFFEE

05: Which artists do you like most?

WINDSOR MC CAY, MAURICE SENDAK, RICHARD SCARRY, MARC BOUTAVANT, SHINZI KATOH, OLAF HAJEK, THE BEATLES, TENESSEE WILLIAMS, HERGE, CHRIS WARE, ALFRED HITCHCOCK, FRIEDRICH SCHINKEL, MARTIN SCORSESE, NEIL YOUNG, WEGEE,... WALT DISNEY

06: What do you think of yourself?

WE SHOULD LOOSE WEIGHT!

07: Can you tell us about what you always dream of doing?

REBUILDING CONEY ISLAND IN BERLIN, WRITING A BOOK (R.) DESIGNING CHILDREN'S TOYS, GAMES & BOOKS, OPENING MY OWN STORE (J)

08: Could you say something to our readers?

AH ... YES!

Q&A

To: CYPI

Attention: in&out

R.E.: QUESTIONS&ANSWERS

Date: 08/08/09

Who you are?
You can draw something here!

01: What does illustration mean to you? How do you define this term?

illustration = drawing, Painting, sketching, doodle, fine Art?

PICTURE

02: Have you ever thought of putting your works into commercial use?

Most of my works are Commercial use....

03: What is your favorite? Please give me six names.

 ① Frasier cake from Paul | ② high heels | ③ Tea time with girl friends | ④ bags... lot of bags | ⑤ Film & Music always can change my mood | ⑥

TEA

04: What do you resent most? Please give me six names.

RUDE PEOPLE ①, cheese ② ew www, Snake ③, lizard ④, The sound of Baby crying drive me mad ⑤, Global warming ⑥

05: Which artists do you like most?

Sean Freeman, Emily forgot, Si Scott, Alex Trochut, Erin Petson,

06: What do you think of yourself?

i think I'm not a bad person, I'm working hard and love shopping

I think I'm too short and getting older now... will have to work on getting younger look

07: Can you tell us about what you always dream of doing?

When I was young - I dream to be a doctor and happily ever after

when I was teenager - I dream to be Interior designer and fall in love

when I was 2M2 - I dream to be Illustrator and have a fun single life

when I am now 28 - ~~illustra~~ my dream are more simple, just to be happy & healthy

08: Could you say something to our readers?

Thank you for looking at my works, I hope you like what you see.

Send me email for feedback (even if you don't like it), say hello or general chit chat.

I love reading letter & Postcard ♥ too :)

Q&A

To: CYPI
Attention: in&out
R.E.: QUESTIONS&ANSWERS
Date: 08/08/09

01: What does illustration mean to you? How do you define this term?

My job! Art works that order from clients...

02: Have you ever thought of putting your works into commercial use?

Yes ♥ ♥ ♥ ♥

03: What is your favorite? Please give me six names.

Time ... being with my boyfriend ... creating something, farming ... napping, and dreaming ♥ ♥

04: What do you resent most? Please give me six names.

Remark of the Prime Minister in Japan.

05: Which artists do you like most?

Fornasetti

06: What do you think of yourself?

Normal

07: Can you tell us about what you always dream of doing?

Own my factory!

08: Could you say something to our readers?

Breathe deeply.

08-AUG-2009 00:26   FROM:

TO: 00AL...

Q&A

To: CYPI
Attention: in&out
R.E.:   QUESTIONS&ANSWERS
Date: 08/08/09

01: What does illustration mean to you? How do you define this term?

Storytelling, playing and giving shape to words + ideas.

02: Have you ever thought of putting your works into commercial use?

Have done it many, many times!   £ KERR Ching

03: What is your favorite? Please give me six names.

· Teatime at 4pm!

· BURIAL (Dubstep! ♥)

· Hiking in mysterious landscapes

· Ponies
· Tinchy Stryder
· Writing and receiving letters

04: What do you resent most? Please give me six names.

· Dogs with bad breath = all dogs.
· Snotty nose in winter
· good things coming to an end and people expecting you to be mature about it.
· TOMATOS

05: Which artists do you like most?

Punchdrunk - collective (theatre + performance)

· Rothko

· Eva Hesse (sculptor)

Michelangelo SISTINE CHAPEL!

→ ⊙ Marcel Duchamps

MIKE NELSON contemporary british installation artist.

06: What do you think of yourself?

Internationally Renowned Illusionists

NO MORE WORRIES. 100% GUARANTEED.
your problem is our business.

07: Can you tell us about what you always dream of doing?

Magnetism. Performance. Clairvoyance.

08: Could you say something to our readers?

IF YOU ONLY HAVE 2 OPTIONS, GO FOR THE THIRD.

Q&A

To: CYPI
Attention: in&out
R.E.: QUESTIONS&ANSWERS
Date: 08/08/09

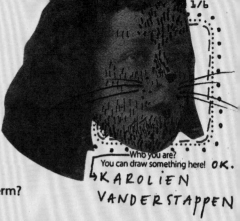

1/6

Who you are?
You can draw something here! OK.
→KAROLIEN VANDERSTAPPEN

01: What does illustration mean to you? How do you define this term?

ILLUSTRATION = SENSATION
(= love)

02: Have you ever thought of putting your works into commercial use?

YES.

03: What is your favorite? Please give me six names.

YVES-KLEIN-BLUE / TO ATTACK OLD MAGAZINES WITH
SCISSORS / CATS / SUN / A DANCING NIGHT + LONG SLEEP
AFTER, LONGER THAN A GIANT / TEA-TIME + READING
                                                    BOOKS

04: What do you resent most? Please give me six names.

Poeha!

NICOLE KRAUSS   = ♥
+

05: Which artists do you like most? AMELIE NOTHOMB, JONATHAN SAFRAN FOER
HENRY DARGER, TAMARA DE LEMPICKA, CHARLOTTE
DADA, MIRANDA JULY THE JANFAMILY, AUDREY CALLEJA,   SALOMON
GOSIA MACHON, SARA FANELLI, DAVID SHRIGLEY, MARCEL
                                                    BROODTHAERS

06: What do you think of yourself?

I THINK I HAVE A LOT OF SHOES

07: Can you tell us about what you always dream of doing?

THE SAME JACKET I JUST GREW OUT OF [AGE ⑦], A BMX [AGE ⑨]
GREEN PEACE [AGE ⑫], A FASHION DESIGNER [AGE ⑮], WRITING
& ILLUSTRATE STORIES [AGE ⑲], A JOB [AGE ㉔], A DRIVERS LICENSE
[AGE ㉖], TO FEEL LUCKY, HAPPY +
LOVE, BEATS OF LOVE / LOVE / LOVE,
BEATS OF LOOŌOVE! [AGE ㉗]
(= illustration) X KARO-
                    LIEN

08: Could you say something to our readers?

HELLO,

come &
sing this
song!

+ YOU HAVE A NICE
HAIRCUT.

Q&A

To: CYPI
Attention: in&out
R.E.:   QUESTIONS&ANSWERS
Date: 08/08/09

01: What does illustration mean to you? How do you define this term?

THE **THRILL** OF CREATING SOMETHING NEW.
(and getting loads of compliments ;)

ILLUSTRATION IS... HM... DECORATIVE ART?

02: Have you ever thought of putting your works into commercial use?

IF DOING WHAT I LOVE MAKES ME RICH, **okay!**

03: What is your favorite? Please give me six names.

ARTWORK FOR : RÓISÍN MURPHY, PALOMA FAITH, SELAH SUE, NIKKA COSTA.
PRADA. A GMAIL THEME.

04: What do you resent most? Please give me six names.

....?

05: Which artists do you like most?

MasaKi   VANIA   sam weber
audrey kawasaki   HENRI   yellena james
MERIJN HOS
TAMARA MULLER   Parra   peter jeroense
LAURA LAINE   SABINE pieper

06: What do you think of yourself?

THAT DEPENDS ON THE  I'M IN.

07: Can you tell us about what you always dream of doing?

THIN KING **BIG**

08: Could you say something to our readers?

Q&A

To: CYPI
Attention: in&out
R.E.:   QUESTIONS&ANSWERS
Date: 08/08/09

Who you are?
You can draw something here!

01: What does illustration mean to you? How do you define this term?

COMMERCIAL

02: Have you ever thought of putting your works into commercial use?

YES

03: What is your favorite? Please give me six names.

CATS / GIRL WITH THE LONELIEST EYES / NIGHT LIFE
EARLY MORNING / EATING / DRINKING

04: What do you resent most? Please give me six names.

HAUGHTINESS

05: Which artists do you like most?

ALBRECHT DÜRER / HANS BALDUNG GRIEN
LUCAS CRANACH / INGRES / PAUL DELVAUX
TAMARA DE LEMPICKA / AUBREY BEARDSLEY / AYAO YAMANA

06: What do you think of yourself?

INDOOR

07: Can you tell us about what you always dream of doing?

EXPLORATION

08: Could you say something to our readers?

USE PENCIL

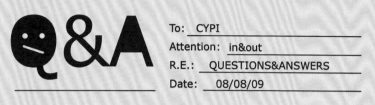

To: ___CYPI_____

Attention: __in&out_____

R.E.: ___QUESTIONS&ANSWERS__

Date: ___08/08/09_____

Who you are?
You can draw something here!

01: What does illustration mean to you? How do you define this term?

Illustration means to transfer what's in my head into another medium.

02: Have you ever thought of putting your works into commercial use?

THAT IS WHAT I ALWAYS DO.

03: What is your favorite? Please give me six names.

noody my dog, sunlight, greenery, old junks, texture, food.

04: What do you resent most? Please give me six names.

BAD FOOD! SPOILED KIDS!

05: Which artists do you like most?

Mark Ryden, Nagi Noda, Gustav Klimt, Alexander McQueen and the mother nature.

06: What do you think of yourself?

fat & lazy.

07: Can you tell us about what you always dream of doing?

MONEY & ENDLESS HOLIDAY.

08: Could you say something to our readers?

FROM: FILIP PAGOWSKI

Q&A

To: CYPI
Attention: Illustrate in&out
R.E.: QUESTIONS&ANSWERS
Date: 08/08/09

Who you are?
You can draw something here!

01: What does illustration mean to you? How do you define this term?

UNFORTUNATELY, NOT MUCH. USUALLY THE CLIENTS DON'T RESPECT IT.... SO I STOPPED CARING ABOUT IT TOO.

02: Have you ever thought of putting your works into commercial use?

ILLUSTRATION IS A COMMERCIAL VENUE. ONE ILLUSTRATES FOR ARTICLES, BOOKS, ADVERTISMENTS, ETC...

03: What is your favorite? Please give me six names.

NATURE, TRAVELING, SKIING, SLEEPING, BEAUTIFUL WOMEN, GOOD FOOD....

04: What do you resent most? Please give me six names.

BORING JOBS, UNEDUCATED ART DIRECTORS, ARROGANT PEOPLE, POLLUTION, GREED, IMPATIENCE....

05: Which artists do you like most?

SAUL STEINBERG
ANTONIO TAPIES
CASPAR DAVID FRIEDRICH
DAVID SMITHSON

06: What do you think of yourself?

THAT I SHOULD WORK HARDER. I PLAY TOO MUCH :-)

07: Can you tell us about what you always dream of doing?

I DREAM OF BEING AN ARCHITECT, A MOVIE DIRECTOR, A MUSICIAN, A SALSA DANCER AND A FOOTBALL PLAYER.

08: Could you say something to our readers?

BE SUSPICIOUS OF ILLUSTRATION!

Q&A

To: CYPI
Attention: Illustrate in&out
R.E.: QUESTIONS&ANSWERS
Date: 08/08/09

JESSE AUER-SALO

Who you are?
You can draw something here!

01: What does illustration mean to you? How do you define this term?

I THINK IT'S SOMETHING THAT'S IN BETWEEN ART
AND DESIGN... BUT IT CAN ALSO BE SIMPLY
ART OR DESIGN. THAT IS THE BEAUTY OF IT.

02: Have you ever thought of putting your works into commercial use?

I'M CONSIDERING ILLUSTRATING AS SOMETHING
THAT HAS A POTENTIAL TO ADAPT ITSELF INTO A
~~SOMETHING~~ NEW. THIS GOES TO COMMERCIAL WORK
(ENVIRONMENT)   AS WELL!

03: What is your favorite? Please give me six names.

BLACK, WHITE, GREY,
DARK, LIGHT, SHADOW.

04: What do you resent most? Please give me six names.

PINK, TURQUOISE, MUSTARD YELLOW
HATE, GREED, SHITFACE

05: Which artists do you like most?

JAN ŠVANKMAJER, BAS JAN ADER, HELMUT NEWTON,
MATTHEW BARNEY, OLAF BREUNING, URS FISCHER,
ALLEN JONES, JEFF KOONS, MARC QUINN ETC...

06: What do you think of yourself?

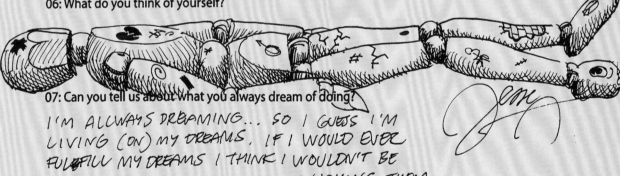

07: Can you tell us about what you always dream of doing?

I'M ALWAYS DREAMING... SO I GUESS I'M
LIVING (ON) MY DREAMS. IF I WOULD EVER
~~FULL~~FILL MY DREAMS I THINK I WOULDN'T BE
ENJOYING THEM
08: Could you say something to our readers? ~~ANYMORE~~

DON'T WORRY, BE HAPPY. BUT ALSO WORRY ONCE IN
A WHILE... IT JUST MEANS THAT YOU CAN
~~ALSO~~ LEAVE YOUR COMFORT ZONE JUST FOR A MINUTE.

(ALSO
IT'S ~~DANGER~~ GOOD
TO STEP BACK
AND SEE THINGS
FROM OTHER
PERSPECTIVE

EDITOR'S NOTES

Birth of This Book

The illustration profession has experienced rapid changes in recent years. Illustrators used to be employed by graphic designers, totally respecting the designers' concepts in the creative process. There was little direct communication between illustrators and clients. However, nowadays, with the development of the illustration industry, clients have a profound understanding of the artists' styles, and tend to give commissions to the illustrators directly. Thanks to this change, the role which the illustrators are playing have become more diversified, functioning as art director, graphic designer, visual effects supervisor, and artist at the same time. It is believed that the following years will witness a closer connection between the illustrators and commerce. They are no longer painters drawing quietly in their studios, but stars who are greatly admired by the public. On the other hand, some illustrators will evolve into artists and be represented by art agencies.

This book is originally intended to share with more readers the works, creative process and commercial approaches of some big names in the illustration industry.

Here, we want to extend sincere thanks to Nie Youjia, who has made enormous contributions to this book, and to Marcos Chin, who is a pride for the illustration profession and a favor of mainstream media. When asked how to introduce him in this afterword, he replies, "Just call me an illustrator. That's enough!" His passions about this profession deserve respects. In addition, we also have to thank Keiichi Tanaami, who has offered a wealth of treasured advices, as well as all the others who have contributed to this book!

Illustrators In & Out
What Moves Them and How They Move Art

Author: Youjia Nie
Project Editor: Jean Chao
English Editors: Fiona Wang, Dora Ding
Translator: Coral Yee
Copy Editor: Lee Perkins
Book Designer: Yuhai Zhang

First published in the United Kingdom in 2011 by CYPI PRESS

Add: 79 College Road, Harrow Middlesex, HA1 1BD, UK
Tel: +44(0)20 3178 7279
Fax: +44(0)19 2345 0465
E-mail: sales@cypi.net editor@cypi.net
Website: www.cypi.co.uk
ISBN: 978-0-9562880-9-7

Printed in China